THE REVELATION OF ST. JOHN

NEW TESTAMENT FOR SPIRITUAL READING

Edited by

John L. McKenzie

THE REVELATION
OF ST. JOHN

Volume I

EDUARD SCHICK

HERDER AND HERDER

1971
HERDER AND HERDER NEW YORK
232 Madison Avenue, New York 10016

Original edition: *Die Offenbarung des hl. Johannes,* from the series *Geistliche Schriftlesung,* edited by Wolfgang Trilling with the cooperation of Karl Hermann Schelkle and Heinz Schürmann, Düsseldorf, Patmos-Verlag, 1970.

Translated by Werner Kruppa.

Nihil Obstat: JOHN M. T. BARTON, STD, LSS, Censor
Imprimatur: ✠ VICTOR GUAZZELLI, Vic. Gen.
Westminster, 18 June 1971

PREFACE

The book of Revelation (or "Apocalypse," a Greek word which means revelation) is a book about which every biblical interpreter knows he will be asked sooner or later. If the commentary of Eduard Schick does nothing more than divert some of these inquiries, it will have served Schick's colleagues very well. The interpreter does not like inquiries about Revelation not just because the book is obscure, but rather because the obscurity is not what the inquirer thinks it is. Revelation is the only prolonged example in the New Testament of a type of writing which was quite common both in late Judaism and in early Christianity, a type to which we give the name apocalyptic literature. One who studies the type can answer most questions by references to other examples of the type; but this is hardly possible for that person who is known as "the general reader." The task which Schick has set himself is not easy. I believe he has carried it off with distinction, but "the general reader" is very hard to please when he inquires about the book of Revelation.

The pre-exilic prophets of the Old Testament spoke to a people who had the power of decision. Whether Israel survived or not depended on their own moral actions. Therefore the prophets could address to them warnings, rebukes, and promises; the people could determine whether the words of the prophets were fulfilled or not. Apocalyptic literature arose in a people who no longer had the power of self-determination. They were a small people lost in a vast empire; they were the victims of history rather than its agents, and what happened to them would be determined by others. Apocalyptic literature is in a sense a flight

v

from history. Since its writers and readers have no power over
their own destiny, they invoke the power of God on their side.
Since no historical force appears which can meet the great world
powers on equal terms, they dream of an event which is trans-
historical and is not the product of the historical forces which
we experience. They dream of the direct intervention of God
in history.

This intervention, naturally, is conceived as occurring in the
near future; but the near future is carefully disguised under
cryptic images and symbols. Very probably these images and
symbols were not as cryptic for the original readers as they are
for modern readers. But they have had the effect that later
readers, beginning in early Christianity, have regarded apocalyptic literature as a prediction of future history, and they have
studied it carefully to see whether its signs are fulfilled in their
own times. The signs are so obscure, often so grotesque, that it
takes little imagination to find them in any historical period of
stress and upheaval. The locusts and the dragon with seven heads
and ten horns can be found in most recent history; and many
of the Reformers identified the Great Whore of Babylon with
the Papacy; the author meant Rome, but the Papacy was scarcely
within his view. A device not employed in Revelation was to
attribute the prediction to some figure of remote antiquity such
as Enoch, who appears in some of the more important Jewish
apocalyptic books.

The entire search, as I have indicated, is the search for an act
of God in history in which the searchers feel that they can play
no effective part. The modern interpreter neither shares the help-
less feeling of later Judaism and some early Christians nor
believes that such a search can be fruitful. He believes that the
key to the understanding of Revelation is a knowledge of the
contemporary history which the writer has hidden under his
images and symbols. It is the history contemporary with the

writer which the writer interprets, not the apocalyptic act of God
in the end time.

But does the modern interpreter really think that the apocalyptic interpretation of history is valid and meaningful for himself and his contemporaries? And does he really expect the
apocalyptic act of God? To answer the last question first, it
would be a bold, even heedless interpreter who would say that
he can surely predict what God will or will not do. As for the
apocalyptic interpretation of history, I think most interpreters
would give a qualified answer. Even if one does indeed expect
an apocalyptic end, one can hardly count on it as a solution of
contemporary problems. The apocalyptic end does not so much
solve problems as end the process in which the problems occur.
One fears that apocalyptic expectation can turn into an abdication
of personal and group responsibility for contemporary problems.
One's awareness of this danger may suggest that no emphasis
be laid on ancient apocalyptic thought; and this suggestion is
strengthened by the fact that almost all apocalyptic schools of
thought within the history of Christianity have been aberrations.
At the same time, one realizes that the church and the nations
have often been blind to the clear approach of disaster. We cannot be sure that apocalyptic thinking would have alerted them
to the approach of disaster.

Apocalyptic literature has contributed much to the Christian
art of medieval and Renaissance times. Pieter Brueghel and
Albrecht Dürer have captured the vivid details of Revelation in
frightening and disgusting representations. Apocalyptic literature
has also contributed to some of the more frightening and disgusting manifestations of the Christian ethos. Revelation, like
much Jewish apocalyptic literature, draws a clear line between
good and evil. It spares no pain in portraying the odiousness of
evil and the hideous punishments which God inflicts upon evil.
The good have often nourished their vindictiveness against their

wicked oppressors from apocalyptic images. They have forgotten that all men stand under the need of redemption.

The interpreter ultimately deals with Revelation as an expression of the biblical belief that history stands under the judgment of God, and stands under this judgment constantly. The judgment is manifested in more subtle ways than the apocalyptic writers describe, and it does not make as sharp a distinction between the good and the wicked as the apocalyptic writers make. But belief in this judgment is basic in Christian faith. Possibly the apocalyptic expression of this faith is not always sympathetic; and in modern times it cuts rather sharply across much of our patterns of thought. This may be due not only to its exaggerated imagery; perhaps we have not the same deep faith in the judgments of God in history, and we may be slow to recognize and accept them. Possibly what we retain from apocalyptic literature is its most dangerous feature, its vindictiveness. But Revelation has always spoken loudly to Christians in times of crisis; and it is most unlikely that it will cease to speak as the modern crisis mounts. The mistake would be to take it as the sole and final interpretation of history.

JOHN L. MCKENZIE

INTRODUCTION

The Secret of History

The entire Biblical revelation, beginning with the primeval history of Genesis up to Revelation in the New Testament, bears witness to God's compassionate actions towards the world and humanity; its subject is the *history of salvation*. It starts with creation, a beginning inaugurated by God, and is set towards a final goal of consummation which the creator has appointed for his work from eternity and towards which he guides it through time with unerring certainty. This makes the historical interpretation of Scriptures radically theological and eschatological, that is to say, it is totally oriented towards the divinely appointed beginning and end of all history. Correspondingly, its portrayal commences with the primeval beginning and ends with a presentation which would like to convey an idea of the final situation; but because the consummated state reaches into the transcendental sphere of divine existence it can only be illustrated analogically, that is, with the aid of comparisons and images taken from the world of our experience, which means that it cannot be described immediately. This endeavor to anticipate the end of the provisional structure of the world and the final, consummated and eternal mode of existence emerging from it, at least by analogical images, corresponds to a special literary genre, the so-called apocalyptic literature as which the last book of the Biblical canon classifies itself with its first word, *apokalypsis*.

This *literary genre* gained its initial impulse from the prophetic writings of the Old Testament, richly developed above all in the two pre-Christian centuries; we find traces of it already in Isaiah (Kings 24–27), Ezekiel (40–48), Zechariah (9–14)—texts which give much latitude to the eschatological perspective—in the Book of Daniel it has finally developed into a mode of writing which permeates and molds the entire work. The time of distress in the epoch of the Maccabees strengthened the interest in the eschatological orientation of historical interpretation; following Daniel, there appeared up to about the beginning of the 2nd century A.D. numerous Jewish (apocryphal) apocalyptic works.

In the New Testament John's Revelation stands alone as a book exclusively apocalyptic in content and form; however, there are other isolated pieces, scattered over the entire New Testament, which can be classified as apocalyptic; they indicate that the original Christian propagation, the recording and transmission of Jesus' preaching, has throughout made use of this literary genre among others. Moreover, the Revelation of John was the occasion of many an imitation in early Christian literature right into the 2nd century; these are partly only Christian revisions of Jewish texts; as a later masterpiece of this genre one could classify Dante's *Divine Comedy*.

John's Revelation is still aware of the fundamental link between the apocalypse and Old Testament *prophecy*; its author calls himself a prophet (10:11; 22:9) and he characterizes his work as a prophetic book (1:3; 22:7–10). The prophets of Israel were leaders of the chosen people, commissioned by God and appearing especially in critical epochs of its history; their guidance and warnings, admonitions and comfort again and again gave the people the right orientation on the path of salvation-history; the glimpse of the coming, final rescue, the time of salvation, naturally played a special role as a basis to their reassuring sermons; in this way, prophecy, the prediction of the future, which by no means was the immediate or even the essential task of the prophet, found a place in their preaching.

Like the writings of the prophets of the Old Testament, John's Revelation, a prophetic book in its over-all intention, also has for aim to impart guidance, strength and consolation to the Church of the time, especially to the communities in the Roman province of Asia Minor in the situation of the moment. Its intention is therefore hortative; the illustrations of the end of time themselves are added as motives for encouragement. The final outcome and goal gives to all contemporary history its meaning and elucidation; what is final gives one the confidence, strength and willingness to endure what is fleeting. For this reason the Revelation traces all lines from what is passing and provisional to the final eternity of the consummation of salvation-history.

The *form of presentation* to this end is a series of allegorical-symbolic picture-compositions, that is, not a language of concepts but of images. This circumstance increases considerably the difficulty of the modern reader in understanding the work. The results of scholarship, especially in recent times, into the late Jewish religious trends in apocalyptic literature, have provided the means and presuppositions of finding one's way better in this type of writing. The Jewish apocalypse works with traditional metaphorical themes whose basic elements are taken from the Old Testament; to these are added themes from a broader, extra-Biblical stream of popular Jewish tradition into which conceptual elements of a mythical character, gleaned from Israel's surrounding pagan world, had also been woven. To know the origin of the metaphorical elements and to identify their stable use in expressing a fixed symbolic content (fixed symbolic values of numbers, colors, natural processes, animals, peoples, cities) is an aid in understanding the meaning. Moreover, by means of the strikingly frequent use of the comparative particle " as," John's Revelation itself draws attention to the fact that it is in no way its aim to describe historical processes, but that it seeks by comparisons (analogically) in its images to give an insight into a reality which being inaccessible to human experience is therefore in a certain sense unutterable. It, therefore, does not depict the actual course of future earthly events, it does not offer a chronological sequence of the end of history, rather it interprets the final meaning of the entire course of history, as well as especially singled out contemporary processes, from the standpoint of the absolute reality of God which, though transcending history, lies at its root and leads it to its goal.

Externally, John's Revelation differs from the writings of the same type in late Judaism by its pleasant sobriety and relatively lucid arrangement of the individual images and of the over-all composition. This characteristic is connected with its *origin*. Unlike the latter, it was not composed at the writing desk as a work of art; it does not depict something fabricated, rather something experienced; it endeavors in the traditional garb, and with the traditional means of the apocalypse, to give intelligible expression to actual visionary experiences in which the Seer, in a prophetic-ecstatic state, was instructed by Christ about the history of his Church. The sequence of images reveals the kernel impetus of the course of world history after the redemptive act of Christ: the militant antagonism, never relaxed and at times intensified especially towards the end of time, between God's kingdom already established in the world by Christ and the reign of Satan which was indeed already basically broken by him but offers resistance still. Whatever Christians experience from time to time in and through the world is at root characterized by this antagonism flowing in the background through all earthly history, whereby the divine history of salvation is brought to its goal by combat.

The isle of Patmos is named as the *place* of this revelatory experience, whither the recipient of the Revelation had been banished because of his faith and apostolic activity (1:9). As he is evidently known to the first addressees and a person of acknowledged authority, the Seer calls himself by his first name only, John. Although the Revelation contains no further clues which might help in exactly fixing the *author's* identity, it is the verdict of the unbiased tradition of the 2nd century that it is the Apostle John (witnesses: Justin, Irenaeus, Clement of Alexandria, Origen; Muratorian fragments; anti-Marcionitic prologue of Luke); not till an uncertainty with regard to Revelation arose as a result of an abuse of the book by Chiliastic fanatics was this originally unanimous tradition disrupted from the 3rd century onward.

The actual *occasion* for this apocalypse, which with its letter-type introduction (1:1–8), the inserted letters to the seven churches (2:1–3:22) and the letter-type conclusion (22:21) has the appearance of an epistle, was an already marked persecution of Christians; its primary *aim* was spiritually to prepare the afflicted Churches of Asia Minor for this time of trial and to encourage them, in the light of the glory of the proffered prize of victory, to a witness of suffering and, if necessary, death.

As to the *time* of its composition, the oldest traditional testimony (Irenaeus, *Against the Heresies*) cites the reign of the emperor Domitian (81–96 A.D.); he took the refusal of the Christians to take part in the emperor-cult as an occasion for the first persecution of Christians in 95/96 which reached beyond the residential city of Rome; this fits in with the fact that Revelation presupposes the imminent threat of a persecution of Christians in Asia Minor.

The *interpretation* must set out from this concrete occasion and purpose even though the contents and meaning of Revelation, as its execution shows, is not limited to rendering guidance for the uniqueness of the historical moment. In this prophetic book the history of the end is put at the service of contemporary history and contemporary history in turn is in manifold traits woven into the images of the end. The delineations of the chapters 13; 17 : 1–19 : 20 are indeed disguised in symbols. Nevertheless the Roman empire, its capital Rome, the emperor-cult are readily recognizable. However, within the framework of the entire composition such contemporary perspectives widen into supratemporal symbols acquiring thereby a typical significance as indeed in reality the central mystery of history, the hostility between the kingdom of God and the usurped power of his foe comes to light in the ever-changing contemporary forms of appearance. Consequently every single historical expression of this process is suitable to illustrate this decisive combat which flows through all world history but remains essentially the same; its phases therefore can be depicted in Revelation in such a way that the portrayal gives the impression of a repetition of processes described earlier which indeed increase in intensity as the end draws nearer but remain substantially the same.

This knowledge which comprises the basic structural law of Revelation will by itself rule out the misunderstanding that the sequence of scenes illustrate an actual historical course of events from which one could without further ado discern how near the world has come to its end. It is not the object of Revelation, nor can it be its object (cf. Mk. 13 : 32; Lk. 17 : 20f.), to give clues for the exact determination of the end of time with the coming of Christ; it intends solely to clarify the total character of the final time, that is, the epoch between the first and the second coming of Christ, so that the Church of Christ would be prepared by virtue of this insight to endure the occasional distressing trials to its faith within the transitory order of earthly history and so to prove herself in the firm conviction that the returning Lord will say the last word on world history, on all epochs, on all who have lived in them and have become responsible by their collaboration. This certainty which supports the entire book as an all-pervading consoling theme is underlined by the frequent repetition of time-specification such as " I will come to you soon " (2:16; 3:11; 22:7. 12. 20) and " the time is near " (1:3; 22:10) which as such within Revelation no more mean to fix the concrete point of " when " than the images in this book mean to give a picture of the concrete manner of the "how "; the certainty of the " that " alone is made urgent and authentic by the foreshortened time-perspective, a prophetic device common also to the Old Testament.

The *theological meaning* of Revelation emerges from its main theme which is no different from the central subject of Jesus' teaching in the synoptic gospels: the kingdom of God, its destiny and its victory in history. This is illustrated by the multiplicity and forcefulness of the images: beginning with its eternal origin (4:1-11) through its establishment in the midst of the history of mankind (5:1-14; 12:1-6) and its destiny in the history of the world (12:13-13:18) up to its final breakthrough (19:11-20:15) and its appearance in a consummated form on earth (21:1-22:5).

As the prophecy unfolds, sublime individual images are drawn up in which all the articles of the apostolic creed appear with the aid of an impressive pictorial theology interpreted originally and fundamentally: the doctrine of God, in a narrower sense (4:1-11), the doctrine of the Redeemer and of redemption (1:5-8. 12-19; 5:6-14; 12:1-6; 14:1-5; 19:11-21; 20:4-6), the doctrine of the Holy Spirit (1:4; 2:7. 17 etc.; 4:5; 5:6; 14:13; 22:17), the doctrine of the Church (1:5f.; 1:20; 2:1-3.22; 7:1-8; 12:13-17), the communion of saints (6:9-11; 8:3-5), the resurrection of the body and eternal life (4:10f.; 7:9-17; 14:14-20; 19:17; 20:15; 21:1-22:5).

Revelation therefore offers a comprehensive and illustrated outline of the entire Christian teaching concerning salvation, organically arranged and built into a great framework of the eschatologically determined history of God with humanity; it follows its course in the foreground phases of history in the light of the preter- and supernatural forces at work in them and always with a view to the final goal which God has set for his creation and towards which he will guide it through every confusion. The last book of God's revelation is the climax and the crowning outcome of the "eternal gospel" (14:6) beginning with the epoch of promise in the Old Testament up to its final perfect fulfillment.

The *structure* of Revelation is relatively lucid. It gives its own division into two parts; the Seer is shown the truth and is requested to write down " what is " and " what is to take place hereafter " (1:19).

OUTLINE

THE INTRODUCTION (1 : 1–20)

   I. Caption and beatitude (1 : 1–3)
   II. The epistolary address (1 : 4–8)
   III. The vocation-vision (1 : 9–20)

Part I : The Contemporary State of the Church (2 : 1—3 : 22)

THE SEVEN LETTERS (2 : 1—3 : 22)

   I. Letter to the church in Ephesus (2 : 1–7)
   II. Letter to the church in Smyrna (2 : 8–11)
   III. Letter to the church in Pergamum (2 : 12–17)
   IV. Letter to the church in Thyatira (2 : 18–29)
   V. Letter to the church in Sardis (3 : 1–6)
   VI. Letter to the church in Philadelphia (3 : 7–13)
   VII. Letter to the church in Laodicea (3 : 14–22)

Part II : The Prophecy of the Future of the Church up to the Final Consummation (4 : 1—22 : 5)

INTRODUCTION : THE SOVEREIGN LORD AND THE TRANSFER OF POWER TO THE LAMB (4 : 1—5 : 14)

   I. The vision of God's throne room (4 : 1–11)
   II. The vision of the transfer of power to the Lamb (5 : 1–14)

THE VISIONS OF THE SEALS (6 : 1—8 : 1)

   I. The first four seals (6 : 1–8)
   II. The fifth seal (6 : 9–11)
   III. The sixth seal (6 : 12–17)

THE INTRODUCTION (1:1-20)

Caption and Beatitude (1:1-3)

[1]The revelation of Jesus Christ, which God gave him to show to his servants what must soon take place; and he made it known by sending his angel to his servant John, . . .

The last book of the New Testament canon calls itself an "apocalypse," that is to say, it wishes to reveal realities which are not accessible to man either by nature, experience or reflection but can only come to his knowledge by way of revelation. In the preparatory phase to the time of salvation God commanded his prophets to tell his chosen people from time to time what he had in mind in their regard, how they were to interpret their history; at the apex of the time of salvation, " he has spoken to us by a Son. . . . He reflects the glory of God and bears the very stamp of his nature, upholding the universe by his word of power " (Heb. 1:2f.).

One must be called to be a prophet; as in the old Covenant by Yahweh so the New Testament prophet John is called by Jesus Christ; from him he also receives what he is to make known ("the revelation of Jesus Christ "). The message of the exalted Jesus like his preaching in his lifetime is revelation of God which he had received from the " Father " (Jn. 12:49; 14:10; 17:8). Like the " word of Yahweh " (Josh. 1:1; Joel 1:1) given to the Old Testament prophets, the New Testament prophecy—as Revelation describes itself (1:3)—is not primarily and essentially a prediction of future happenings in place and time, but a disclosure of divine instructions in the form of warnings, threats

3

and promises referring to a definite historical situation and experience which are intended as a help to their understanding and control. Concrete historical events are thereby always measured against the prime fact, which determines them in content and direction, the necessary dependence of all beings and events on God as coming from him and moving towards him.

From God's point of view the nearest and most distant future is a " soon " (2 Pet. 3:8; Ps. 90 [89]:4). In the prophetic literary genre which usually paints on the surface without a depth-dimension and so above all blurs over the time-perspective the word " soon " pales almost to a symbolic value which expresses the absolute certainty that the event will take place and correspondingly aims at producing a wakeful readiness in those concerned; this associated with the " must," which characterizes the immutable divine plan of salvation which can cope with any opposition, aims at imparting to the addresses of Revelation consolation and encouragement in distress. They are called " his servants " because they recognize God as the absolute Lord of the world and its history and acknowledge him as such for themselves personally. All who share in this faith are thereby addressed also; they are to be " shown " God's plan in regard to the world which no man can discover by himself either through philosophical speculation concerning the reality of things or by reflection into the depths of the self. God's revelation to man comes in quite the opposite way; as we shall see, John went into ecstasy, that is to say, God's spirit lifted him outside the confines of the self, its possibilities and limits, that he might recognize the intentions and ways of God with the world and man which in this state of being-outside-himself he is shown in manifold images (" all that he saw," 1:3) to be then passed on to the Church.

Hence what he offers in his writing is revelation; this fact needs a guarantee. This is done by recording the way in which

he obtained it: God – Jesus – an angel – John; through this traditional chain, which follows the reliability of the source down to
the reliability of the last link, the contents are secured; moreover,
a very illuminating illustration of the fact that—and why—the
tradition principle alone can be the manner in which revelation
is passed on.

In the line of tradition between Jesus Christ and John an angel
has been inserted as an intermediary. As is often said of Yahweh
in the old Covenant, the Lord, now raised to the throne of the
Father, also calls an angel to his service to deliver a message; the
glory and power of God's essence, not bearable to man in an
immediate vision (cf. Ex. 33:20), makes itself known through
angels in a created disguise (cf. Lk. 2:9); through this reflection
of his glory they are identified as God's messengers.

Angels and demons play a considerable role in Revelation, man
seems to be placed as it were between these spiritual forces and
thereby in the decision between good and evil. It is the task of
the angels of revelation in Revelation to show the Seer the
images as a guarantee that the vision is not a human illusion but
is produced by God; at times too they explain to him the truth
of a symbol which in itself is not easily intelligible.

²... *who bore witness to the word of God and to the testimony
of Jesus Christ, even to all that he saw.*

The task imposed on the "servant" of Jesus is that of witness;
his personality withdraws completely behind this function of
bearing witness. His witness in turn rests on the witness of
Jesus himself who is a "faithful witness" (1:5); his name (an
expression of his nature) is therefore "Faithful and True"
(19:11). He can therefore render reliable witness to the "word
of God" because he knows the Father (Mt. 11:27) and so speak
from an immediate vision of that to which he bears witness

(Jn. 3:11. 31f.); " to bear witness to the truth " (Jn. 18:37) he
went to his death. The "word of God" to which Jesus bears
witness contains both his witness to God and the witness of God
to Jesus (Jn. 5:32. 37; 8:18). As we shall see, Revelation is
even pre-eminently and chiefly an interpretation of the person
and work of Jesus in its significance for world history.

*3a Blessed is he who reads aloud the words of the prophecy, and
blessed are those who hear, and who keep what is written
therein; . . .*

All necessary details as to source, content and type of revelation
as well as its communication and recipient having been stated in
the caption, John concludes his foreword with a beatitude of his
readers and hearers; he presupposes that the " revelation of Jesus
Christ " will be read at divine service to the assembled faithful;
the communication therefore passes through John to the communities. In the reading of the " word of God," recorded by a
chosen witness, his offer of salvation is made effectively present
among the faithful as communication and challenge. For those
who with inner preparedness take it to heart and let it bear fruit
within (cf. Lk. 11:28) is meant the first of the seven beatitudes
of Revelation.

3b . . . for the time is near.

In order to stress the urgency of the summons implied in the
beatitude the warning that the still remaining time is short
stands like an exclamation mark at the end of the foreword. The
" near " resumes the sense of " soon " (1:1). Through the first
coming of Christ time has acquired in itself and for mankind a
new quality of being; in him it was enclosed by eternity; " but
when the time had fully come " (Gal. 4:4) the actual full sense

of all time had been made known (cf. Eph. 1:9f.) which in his second coming will be openly revealed. The time in between no longer possesses a center of gravity; after the " end of the ages " (1 Cor. 10:11) has arrived through him, its significance will lie in its consummation at the dawn of the " day of Jesus Christ " (Phil. 1:6. 10; 2:16) which will know no evening. The admonition to a wakeful readiness and the theme of encouragement and consolation which runs through Revelation permeate one another in this challenge.

The Epistolary Address (1:4–8)

[4a]*John to the seven churches that are in Asia : . . .*

An introduction has been attached to Revelation 1:4–8, as it has been to John's Gospel (Jn. 1:1–18), which in the manner of a prologue announces the theme and isolates in outline some of the motifs. Because John had intended his writing for reading at divine service (1:3) he gives the prologue the traditional form of a letter caption of antiquity: he names the sender and recipient and sends his compliments (cf. the addresses of the New Testament, esp. Jas. 1:1).

The sender calls himself by the first name John without any further additions; this presupposes that he is known to the addressees and possesses authority in the churches of Asia Minor; in 1:1 he had called himself a servant of Jesus Christ as Paul is accustomed to do in the opening of his letters (Rom. 1:1 i.a.; cf. also Jas. 1:1; 2 Pet. 1:1; Jud. 1), he had also emphasized his calling to be a " witness " (1:2). The charge to serve and the willingness to serve are the most prominent characteristics of the person called. As recipients, seven churches of an area of Asia (West Asia Minor) under Roman rule are specified, these are later called by name (1:11). The number seven plays the same role in the construction of Revelation as does the ground-plan in the erection of a building; the seven letters (2:1–3:22) are followed by three further series of seven into which the visions of destiny are ordered: the seven seals (6:1–8:2), the seven trumpets (8:2–11:19), the seven plagues (15:1–16:21). This structure owes its origin to the significance which was attached to the number seven in ancient number-symbolism, it is a sign of what is concluded, of completeness and abundance. Therefore, behind the number seven of Asia Minor's churches appears the totality of communities of Jesus Christ in Asia as in the whole world; the Church of all places and ages is addressed in this book.

4bGrace to you and peace from him who is and who was and who is to come, . . .

The formula of greeting " Grace and peace " can be found in almost all letters of the New Testament; this wording probably has its source in Paul who combined the everyday greeting of the Greek world, *chaire* (greeting), with that of the semitic people, *shalom* (peace), and Christianized them both; grace and peace circumscribe the quintessence of salvation in Jesus Christ. Such a greeting sent by the messenger of Christ posits beyond the wish an effective deed (Mt. 10:12f.; Lk. 10:5f.); the desired salvation becomes reality in those greeted. The power of blessing is therefore expressly transferred at ordination.

But man is never the giver of blessings, always God himself; his name is circumscribed here in three solemn formulae corresponding to the threefold form in which God revealed himself in the history of his revelation. The person of the Father is here exemplified by three predicates of majesty which express God's essence in his transcendence and in his rule over history. The first clearly refers to the revelation of God in the burning thorn bush and the name Yahweh (Ex. 3:14); God is who is always and everywhere present; already in late Judaism the name Yahweh was interpreted as indicating God's eternity and ever-lastingness which is here especially stressed by the additional predicate: "who was." As clearly indicated in the substitution of "who is to come" for "who will be," the third predicate joins the transcendent God to the history of this world in which he will in time reveal himself in the complete fullness of his glory as its director and master. The bow of God's being is here bent widely: from timelessness to the beginning of all created being and the changing events within space and time up to the final point which God will set for it in judgment and consumma-tion.

4c. . . . *and from the seven spirits who are before his throne . . .*

Similarly the fulfillment of the blessing is made dependent on the "seven spirits"; just as the seven communities symbolize the whole Church so the seven spirits symbolize here the fullness of spirit, its perfection without measure or limit (cf. also Is. 11:2). The being "before the throne of God" apparently circumscribes what is later (4:5; 5:6) clarified with the version "the seven spirits of God"; the Holy Spirit is meant here for whom alone the predicate is appropriate: the fullness of spirit, the perfect spirit. It is the same Spirit who also lets the words of their Lord Jesus be heard in the seven churches (cf. 2:7. 11. 17. 29; 3:6. 15. 22).

5a. . . . *and from Jesus Christ the faithful witness, the first born of the dead, and the ruler of kings on earth.*

The second person of the divine trinity, Jesus Christ receives mention only in the third place; and again with three predicates, his appearance as man in humility, his obedience unto death to the task of revelation which his Father charged him with (cf. 1:3) and his glory through resurrection and being raised to the throne of the Father to rule over all powers of the earth, that is, above all his role as saviour is brought to mind here.

The earthly life of Jesus is as a whole characterized as one of bearing witness; he is the revelation of God not only in the sense of information concerning God's being and actions but also as a self-communication of God in the shape of a man to men; not only his word, he himself in his person is the faithful and true (cf. 3:14) discloser. God has offered in him his word, the fullness of his revelation to men and has guaranteed these absolutely, for Jesus Christ is the " word of God " (19:11) in person, and consequently he merits unconditional faith. He is called the " first-born from the dead " (cf. Col. 1:18; 1 Cor. 15:20) because he was the first human being whom death could not hold; and as such he is not the only and last, but the first " of many "; his resurrection is a promise for all, the beginning of a new creation of God (cf. 3:14) in which everything is guided towards rebirth out of transitoriness and death, visibly represented and guaranteed in the reality of the risen One. The glorification of Jesus, beginning visibly with his resurrection, possesses a decisive significance not only for man but for the entire history of the world; exalted to the throne of the Father he has with God assumed dominion over the universe (cf. 4:8 with 5:13f.) and corresponding to the special optics of Revelation, his rule over the politically powerful on earth is given special prominence here (cf. 17:14; 19:16). In the acknowledgement of the sovereignty of Jesus the theme of hope, consolation and encouragement for the Church in persecution is struck up, a theme which is repeated from the beginning and from there again and again.

[5b]*To him who loves us and has freed us from our sins by his blood [6]and made us a kingdom, priests to his God and Father, to him be glory and dominion for ever and ever. Amen.*

The triple declarations of majesty change into a threefold praise of Jesus and his work in which is indicated also what he means for us. (The insertion of the doxology is probably the external reason why the Holy Spirit was named before the Son.) The One exalted to sovereignty has not on that account withdrawn from his own into heights of glorious majesty; he remains one with them in the divine magnitude of his love. With love he also exercises his power over, and for his own, after he had revealed is as man to be a love stronger than death itself (Jn. 15:13; cf. Jn. 3:16). Through giving his life—blood stands here as a symbol of life (cf. Lev. 17:11)—he has won their liberation from the power of sin, a loosening of their guilt before God and thus opened anew for them the path to God which expands into an unsuspected election in which a prophecy of the pre-Christian era (Ex. 19:6) finds its fulfillment. He who has saved us from the power of sin does not make us into subjects but has engaged us as his co-rulers on earth. Wherever his redeemed are, his dominion is present through them in the midst of this world for they know him in faith and follow the example of his love. Wherever the Church is actively present the dominion of God is there working towards that full stature promised in days to come and the Lord of all is in the midst of his community and present in its members in this world although at times the outward appearance, the contempt for, and persecution of his followers throughout the world would lead one to suspect quite the opposite. He who shares in the dominion of the exalted Lord also shares in his eternal priesthood (cf. also 1 Pet. 2:9) which is described as a royal priesthood in the New Testament (Heb. 5:6; 1:17. 21). His priestly service before God consisted in his redemptive death for mankind (Heb. 9:11f.). From the share which the faithful have in his priestly office follows also their adoption of his priestly mentality towards God (Heb. 10:8–10) such as his preparedness to serve as mediator between God and the world (Heb. 5:1f.; 7:24f.). These exalted distinctions give the faithful their confidence in God (Heb. 10:19–21) in the teeth of worldly opposition (cf. Jn. 16:32). The majestic predicates of glory and power which in 1:5 were bestowed on the exalted Lord are in conclusion repeated in a confession-formula as a doxology for him and substantiated by the Hebraic particle of ratification, " Amen."

⁷Behold, he is coming with the clouds; and every eye will see him, every one who pierced him; and all the tribes of the earth will wail on account of him. Even so. Amen.

His glory and power, which are now hidden, will some day in the future flash out before the world; for this Jesus Christ, of whom John is writing, " is coming." That is the proclamation of the book's theme. Whatever may happen, in everything, in the greatest horrors of history even and the most terrible plagues of mankind, as they are later portrayed in apocalyptic imagery, his coming is proclaimed, the world experiences the omen of its judgment. Thus the question of mankind put to the future, if properly put, should not be: what will happen? but: who is coming? With the aid of two images from the Old Testament, the One coming is more closely characterized and the significance of his arrival for the world is announced. The reference to the vision of Daniel, the image of the Son of Man to whom is given universal and eternal dominion (Dan. 7:13f.), characterizes the One coming as the Lord and Judge of the world (cf. Dan. 7:26). The text from Zechariah (12:10), which is quoted in John's gospel as a quotation for reflection in the account of the piercing with the lance (Jn. 19:37), underlines the thought here that he whom all now recognize as their judge is the Crucified. But this insight and the remorse of those who trespassed against him comes too late, the wail of lamentation can only be an expression of the foreseen condemnation. The first coming in baseness leads via Golgotha to the second coming in the glory and the power of the judge of the world. The absolute certainty of this happening is at the end substantiated with a double Yes (Greek and Hebrew).

The Vocation-Vision (1:9–20)

⁹ᵃ*I, John, your brother, who share with you in Jesus the tribulation and the kingdom and the patient endurance . . .*

A prophet does not speak in his own name; he needs to be sent and enabled by God to preach his word. Hence, as in the case of the Old Testament prophets John also receives a special vocation whose circumstances are here described. With the appointment and mission from God, the authority over those on whom this duty is to be discharged is naturally also bestowed; in the same way, such a mission, to which God calls, is as to content and execution independent of human knowledge, insight and of one's own discretion; for the authority of the person called depends as little on his personality as on his competence and aptitude, but on the mission to which he has been called, by virtue of which he can insist that his service be taken seriously and be accepted. For this reason, too, office in the Church does not create, as often is the case in the world, the relationship superior-inferior, for in the Church all have but one master to whom all are subject, Jesus Christ; among themselves they are " brothers " (Mt. 23:8). Thus John also introduces himself to those to whom he turns with his charge from their common master with the appellation " brother," which the first Christians liked to call themselves. With all he shares the same grace of election by God and the same destiny in the world. They have, if indeed still invisibly, already a share in the royal sovereignty of their transfigured master but must, while on earth, share that fate with him which the world had prepared for him (Mt. 10:38f.; 16:24; 24:9; Jn. 15:20; 16:33). " Tribulation " in the world is promised the Church as her normal condition and the experience of history shows that the relaxation of this suffering from outside normally brings with it a decrease in unity and peace within; a common threat, on the contrary, strengthens brotherly ties, and in persecution it ensures that the individual's fidelity to the faith is courageously kept intact by virtue of the hoping expectancy of the coming Lord with whose coming their share in his sovereignty will become a blessed experience.

9b. . . *was on the island called Patmos on account of the word of God and the testimony of Jesus.*

The suffering of John has its special form and reason. He had preached the word of God in the province of Asia where he bore testimony to the salvation offered by God and accomplished by Jesus Christ (cf. Acts 1:8; 4:33; 5:32). In order to close his mouth as missionary and at the same time to deprive the Christian communities of Asia Minor of their support he was banished from the mainland and brought by force to the rocky island of Patmos, 24 square miles in size, situated west of Milet. The first Christian persecution which spread to Asia was under the emperor Domitian in 95/96; here was the first clash between Christianity and the Roman empire on account of the emperor-cult (the demand of divine honors to the genius of the Roman world-empire incorporated by the emperor). It appears that the persecution is not yet in full swing but in the banishment of John it already casts its shadow. By human standards isolated from the Church of the time, the Spirit of God makes him into his special instrument at the place of banishment whereby he himself comes to the aid of the Church of Christ against the opposition of the mighty of the world.

[10a]*I was in the Spirit on the Lord's day* . . .

It happened on the " Lord's day," on a Sunday—the celebration of the first day of the week, the day of Jesus' resurrection, with the Eucharistic banquet had already replaced the Jewish sabbath (Acts 20:7; 1 Cor. 16:2)—that the Spirit of God came over John to make him a prophetic Seer and a preacher of the word of God, which Jesus wanted to communicate to his Church. The ecstatic state in which John experiences his vocation, and then also receives the message in images (visions), is explained by himself as being filled by the Holy Spirit; his human spirit, without losing its own consciousness, is enabled to receive knowledge which is inaccessible to it by nature. The human spirit must first be opened and be borne beyond its possibilities if it is to receive and understand divine revelation; for this reason the ability to believe and the act of faith itself are also an effect of God's Spirit, that is, of Grace.

[10b]*. . . and I heard behind me a loud voice like a trumpet,* [11]*saying, Write what you see in a book and send it to the seven churches : to Ephesus and to Smyrna and to Pergamum and to Thyatira and to Sardis and to Philadelphia and to Laodicea.*

The first vision begins with an auditory experience (audition); a voice behind, not inside, the enraptured prophet, whose sonic strength hits him like a trumpet blast, calls him. It forces him to turn and see who is calling to impart a mission. The experience comes upon him fully unprepared; the mission itself lay outside his field of vision because its execution, from a human point of view, must have seemed impossible; in genuine prophecy there is no physical self-attunement. He is to write down what he will be shown and to send the entries to seven specified churches. Jesus had commanded the apostles to preach the gospel by word of mouth; this charge, we here note, is extended to a preaching by the written word. The word of God, which he is to pass on in writing, he will be shown in images; the language of images was also the preferred mode of preaching of Jesus himself. The word of God can in this way be made not only audible but also can and should be made visible, because seeing, even mere visual representation, is the most impressive and effective mode of acquiring knowledge for mankind. Although the visualization of the supernatural truths of revelation can always only occur in analogical images, and the communication of the revelation must therefore always work with the comparative particle " like," this way, nevertheless, leads more easily and impressively to a deeper understanding than would a pale concept. In the parables of Jesus, as in Revelation, indeed, only an analogical knowledge is acquired in this way; but even the language of spiritual concepts does not immediately reach the content of revelation nor does it lead beyond such analogical knowledge. Even the " word of God " visible to man in the person of Jesus did not show the reality of God immediately to the human spirit, but merely brought it closer by breaking through the sphere of human experience. For the same reason, John too can only pass on what he was shown in the ecstasy by means of visual forms which were his own and, respectively, not unknown to the recipients to whom he must impart what he saw as a message coming from the Lord himself (cf. 2:1; 2:8; 2:12, etc.). We shall see how John forcefully accomplishes this with images and words from the Old Testament with which God " spoke of old to our fathers " (Heb. 1:11).

¹²Then I turned to see the voice that was speaking to me, and on turning I saw seven golden lampstands.

When John turned he experienced his first vision; it shows him, the transfigured Lord Jesus, as he is present in the midst of his Church on earth. One cannot mistake the consoling aspect of this vision for his persecuted Church on earth. The seven golden lampstands are, at the end of the vision (1:20), explained as symbols of the seven churches for which this message is intended. In the temple at Jerusalem the seven-armed, golden lampstand burned as a symbol of the Old Testament people of God. The lamps are of the most precious metal, gold; in Revelation it appears always besides pearls, precious stones and crystal as the raw material of heaven (cf. 21:15. 18. 21). The gold of the lampstands shows here too that the Church as a community of " saints," that is, chosen by, and for God (that is how the Christians are addressed in most of Paul's letters: Rom. 1:7; Cor. 1:2; Phil. 1:1; Col. 1:2), is already here on earth truly linked (cf. Phil. 3:20) with God's heaven and not merely by virtue of a future hope. The inner nature of the Church as the community of Christ, gathered about their exalted Lord to let themselves be animated, directed and judged by him, could not be more clearly and vigorously represented than as it is in this image. Very probably it is also meant to express the mission of the Church in the world; it is reminiscent of Our Lord's saying concerning the lamp on the lampstand (Mt. 5:14-16) and of the similes of the apostles taken from the sphere of light describing the life of Christians in the world.

¹³And in the midst of the lamp stands one like a son of man, clothed with a long robe and with a golden girdle around his breast; ¹⁴his head and his hair were white as white wool, white as snow; his eyes were like a flame of fire, ¹⁵his feet were like

B

burnished bronze, refined as in a furnace, and his voice was like the sound of many waters, . . .

The form in which the Lord is seen in the midst of his Church reminds one again of the " son of man " in Dan. 7 : 13 (cf. 1 : 7); according to the gospels Jesus liked to apply this name to himself to express his Messianic mission; in Daniel the son of man appears as the one to whom " all authority in heaven and earth has been given " (Mt. 28 : 18); the transfigured son of man is the Lord of his Church. The long robe and the golden girdle were the distinctive items of clothing for priests and kings. The authority of the son of man is exercised as it was by the High Priest of Israel in his being mediator between God and man (cf. Heb. 7 : 24f.). The rest of the description also relies on the book of Daniel, that is, on the portrait of the one " ancient of days " (Dan. 7 : 9); the gleaming white is the color of transfiguration. If Revelation simply transfers the figure of the one " ancient of days " onto the " son of man," this means that God himself appears in the glorified Jesus; corresponding then to the model in Daniel the divine traits of eternity and omniscience (" his eyes were like a flame of fire ") are given special prominence in this " son of man." The penetrating look is a prerequisite for the office of judge which is later expressly appropriated to him with the image of the " two-edged sword." The impression of stability and power which the whole apparition exudes is echoed in the description of the feet; hard as precious brass and gleaming with the light of heaven, they illustrate the full authority of the divine victor whom no historical power can impede or turn from his path and to whose judgment all must one day submit. To the super-human and overwhelming figure the voice is also appropriate; its strength is illustrated by the image of a roaring storm-flood, the like of which John had probably experienced in a winter on Patmos (cf. also Ps. 29[28] :

3–5). No one can remain deaf to his voice, his word of command is compelling in its effect.

[16a]. . . *in his right hand he held seven stars, from his mouth issued a sharp two-edged sword, . . .*

As did the emperors and kings of old hold the imperial orb, so the sovereign holds in his right hand as symbol of ruling authority seven stars which at the end of the vision are interpreted as the " angels of the seven churches," that is to say, representatives of God who are charged with the leadership of the churches, namely the superiors who exercise the office of leadership in the name of Jesus. Besides the protection and security which the Lord offers them, this image also symbolizes his sovereignty over them which is clarified further by the sword of judgment issuing from his mouth; responsible to him they will have to render him a strict account—the sword is two-edged—in the coming judgment.

[16b]. . . *and his face was like the sun shining in full strength.* [17]*When I saw him I fell at his feet as though dead. But he laid his right hand upon me, saying, Fear not . . .*

The description concludes with the repeated reference (1 : 14f.) to the supernatural abundance of light which shines from the apparition of the " Lord of glory " (1 Cor. 2 : 8), unbearable to the human eye like a glance into the bright sun at midday. As in the case of the three disciples at the transfiguration of Jesus on the mountain in Galilee (Mt. 17 : 6), John falls to the ground under this impression " as though dead "; man feels himself as annihilated before the revealed essence and power of God (cf. Is. 6 : 5; Ezek. 1 : 28). The Lord brings John to himself again with a consoling phrase with which a disciple is well acquainted as coming from the mouth of his master. Considering the full text of the utterance together with the associated gesture of laying-on of hands, it seems to reach beyond the sense of a mere resuscitation to a deeper significance; for the call is followed by a self-identification and after that John receives a clearly defined mission; evidently he receives the ordination of a prophet by the laying-on of hands.

[17b]*I am the first and the last,* [18]*and the living one; I died and behold I am alive for evermore, and I have the keys of Death and Hades.*

In the self-identification the transfigured Lord ascribes epithets to himself which were previously predicated of God (1:8); like the Father he is eternal, exists before the world, stands above its history and in his sight it will one day come to an end; the " living one " is an Old Testament appellation for God in contrast with dead idols. But then the self-introduction continues with a forceful reference to his incarnation; he has shared human destiny with us even to death itself and has also overcome it for us by his resurrection to eternal life; as a victor over death he has become master of Death's domain and of the dead imprisoned in it. Therefore, right at the beginning of this book which aims to inspire a readiness to profess him even unto death, he appears to all who must die in his name in the incipient persecution as the living promise of life; those who belong to him have found with him and in him the absolute standpoint beyond all real fear, beyond existential fear in the face of death.

[19]*Now write down what you see, what is, and what is to take place hereafter.* [20]*As for the mystery of the seven stars which you saw in my right hand, and of the seven golden lampstands, the seven stars are the angels of the seven churches, and the seven lampstands are the seven churches.*

Equipped for his mission, the prophet's task (1 : 11) is now repeated and exactly defined. He is to record in writing what is shown him in the visions and to send them collectively to the seven churches of Asia Minor and to their superiors (cf. 1 : 16). A clue as to the contents states that he will receive disclosure concerning the present state of the Church (" what is ") and the future course of the history of salvation (" what is to take place hereafter "). This division corresponds to the lay-out of the book.

Present and future as forms of time-experience still remain separate although the inner structure of time has essentially changed with the first coming of the Saviour. Time has become the " final time," not only in the sense that it is totally directed towards his second coming, but more so since the Son of God has bodily entered it, having overcome all time decay in his bodily resurrection, the seed of eternal life has been sown in its transitory course. The eternal future has already begun with the establishment of " God's kingdom " in the world and mankind; it has become the true driving force of world-history on its course towards final fulfillment; then will be revealed what was already present in the final time (cf. Rom. 8 : 18–25).

PART I:

The Contemporary State of the Church
(2:1—3:22)

THE SEVEN LETTERS (2:1—3:22)

These are real letters which make a comment on the special conditions in each of the seven specified churches of Asia Minor; like the other New Testament letters and partly also the Acts they afford concrete insights into the state of the young Church. The historical uniqueness of these seven Christian communities in Revelation is made to reflect phenomena which return always similarly in the Church everywhere; hence the language of the seven letters is symbolic language which transcends the data of that place and time and extends the actuality of the time to that of all time; in the number seven of Christian communities, in which originally the entire Church is symbolized, manifestations of the entire Church of the future are already embodied.

The letters form a unity formally and as to content. All are constructed on the same scheme which here and there varies slightly; all have Jesus Christ as sender who identifies himself at the beginning of each letter with epithets from the vocation-vision (1:9–20) which already anticipate the judgment on the state of the community given subsequently. Commendations, admonitions, warnings culminate each time in the promise of eternal life given under varying images. In the invitation to take to heart what the Spirit has to say to the churches the exhortation of Jesus becomes the exhortation of the Spirit; indeed his Spirit guides his Church on earth (Jn. 14:17. 26; 16:7-15).

As to content, all the letters have the basic idea in common that the transfigured Lord is invisibly present to his Church, takes charge of it, admonishing and guiding, stands by her in

25

difficulties and eternally rewards her loyalty (motif of encouragement and consolation).

Letter to the Church in Ephesus (2:1–7)

1a To the angel of the church in Ephesus write : . . .

The beginnings of the Christian community at Ephesus are linked with significant names. Paul was their founder (Acts 19), Timothy later took charge of them at the request of the apostle (1 Tim. 1:3); old tradition has it that the apostle John stayed there until he died. Ephesus was the largest of the seven cities and situated nearest to the island Patmos; it was the seat of the Roman provincial government; it was of religious importance because of the ancient pilgrim's shrine of the " Artemis of Ephesus " (cf. Acts 19:23–40).

1b . . . the words of him who holds the seven stars in his right hand, and walks among the seven golden lampstands.

The Lord introduces himself to the Church at Ephesus as the One in whose hands she is held and protected; she stands under his authority and under his almighty custody; he is present to his Church as the " living one " (cf. 1:18) and he is close to every single community whose duty it is to reflect the " light of the world " (Jn. 8:12; 9:5; 12:46) " in the darkness " of this world (cf. Jn. 1:5; 3:19), to shine with the light of Christ in this world and for this world; a supernatural description of every local church to the present day, reassuring and disturbing at the same time.

2a I know your works . . .

Present in the community, the exalted Lord knows their outer circumstances as well as their inner state. At least according to the immediate wording (" I know *your* . . ."), the head of the local church gets the credit as also the discredit for her condition; the inner well-being of the community and correspondingly its effectiveness outside depends essentially on this ministry for all and sundry which he must perform in the sight of the Lord undeterred by difficulties from the outside or criticism and opposition from within.

[2b]. . . *your toil and patient endurance, and how you cannot bear evil men but have tested those who call themselves apostles but are not, and found them to be false;* [3]*I know you are enduring patiently and bearing up for my name's sake, and you have not grown weary.*

Christ knows about the loyalty of the church at Ephesus, she has actively and passively proven herself by decisiveness in action and fortitude in suffering. She has also shown alertness and staunchness in her attitude to wandering missionaries who had spread false doctrine. A discernment of spirits (cf. 1 Jn. 4:1) had helped her to part ways with the false " apostle " (cf. 2 Cor. 11:13-15) and uncompromisingly preserve the purity of doctrine and of the Christian life. In such cases what counts is purely and simply the truth which God has entrusted to his Church with his revelation and the way of life he has traced out in it.

[4]*But I have this against you, that you have abandoned the love you had at first.* [5]*Remember then from what you have fallen, repent and do the works you did at first. If not, I will come to you and remove your lampstand from its place, unless you repent.*

The rebuke, which Christ nevertheless cannot spare his community, refers to the fact that in spite of their energetic commitment, their staunch loyalty and fortitude in suffering, that spirit
which alone gives things their soul and makes them valuable in
God's eyes, namely, love, has not remained equally alive in them.
Perhaps it was precisely their activism which was at fault so that
the state of the community in this regard could no longer endure
comparison with a former state; life and work are no longer in
the same measure and with the same pure selflessness of former
times an expression of their link with God and complete devotion
to his glory; instead self-complacency and desire for recognition
seems to have crept into their motives for action; this means a
betrayal of love as God demands it and as the church at Ephesus
gave him at the start. Their present condition then shows a
considerable decline in contrast with former times. Hence they
must be brought back to their senses, to a change of heart and
spirit so that the work of the community once more becomes an
expression of their love of God, that spirit and action are once
more united and that their achievements once more acquire value
before God; otherwise the Lord threatens to sit in judgment on
them by robbing them of his presence and thereby his grace; left
to themselves they cannot endure.

⁶*Yet this you have, you hate the works of the Nicolaitans, which
I also hate.*

As often in case of those who rebuke out of love an encouraging
word follows a reprimand; here it is repetition of the praise
which was already given them for their uncompromising and
firm attitude to the false doctrines; this group probably bears the
name of their ring-leader Nicolaus. The Lord hates their prac-

tices, moral looseness, which they very probably substantiated with their false ideas.

[1]He who has an ear, let him hear what the Spirit says to the churches. To him who conquers I will grant to eat of the tree of life, which is in the paradise of God.

The " victor-text " follows the demand to give attention and heed to the word of God's Spirit, which is the Spirit of Christ. Here we are reminded that a Christian life in the world means battle; he who endures will gain the prize of victory, eternal life, which is paraphrased in the seven letters with varying Biblical imagery similar to the beatitudes in the Sermon on the Mount (Mt. 5 : 3–12); here, as a return to paradise and access to the tree of life whose fruits give eternal life (cf. Gen. 2 : 9; Acts 22 : 2).

Letter to the Church in Smyrna (2 : 8–11)

[8a]And to the angel of the church in Smyrna write : . . .

Smyrna, the old capital city of Lydia, a good harbor and significant commercial center, with a strong colony of Jews, is known in the history of early Christianity above all by the venerable figure of the Bishop Polycarp; his heroic death of witness to Christ (156 A.D.) is impressively portrayed by a contemporary document, the *Martyrium Polykarpi* (about 160 A.D.). He became a victim of the refusal to take part in the emperor-cult which was established in the city by the erection of a temple to the emperor Tiberius (26 A.D.). As far back as 195 A.D. there existed an alliance with Rome which, because it was never broken, earned for the city the honorary title " Smyrna, the loyal." The letter touches on various such local circumstances.

[8b] . . . *The words of the First and the Last, who died and came to life, . . .*

Christ introduces himself here with titles which acknowledge him as the eternal being and the victor also over corporeal death (cf. 1:17). In view of the imminent persecution, in which it is a question of life or death for the faithful in the event of their refusal to take part in the emperor cult, the King of Eternity, superior to all earthly powers, even that of death, gives them confidence and courage with this self-characterization at the start.

[9] . . . *I know your tribulation and your poverty (but you are rich) and the slander of those who say that they are Jews and are not, but are a synagogue of Satan.* [10a]*Do not fear what you are about to suffer.*

In contrast with the excessive self-consciousness at Ephesus the mood in Smyrna seems too modest and depressed; the community has experienced tribulation, contempt and rejection from its surroundings; economic poverty in the midst of a rich businessman's city is the mark of its position and its standing in society; the reputation which the Christians enjoy in public corresponds to this. Responsible for the contempt and slander are chiefly the Jews of Smyrna who in their rejection and opposition to the " Messiah of God " (Lk. 9:20) had gone into the camp of God's foe. The " community of Yahweh " (Num. 16:3) later became a " synagogue of Satan " (cf. Jn. 8:44).

Compared with their antagonists, who may appear rich in the eyes of men, the Christians in Smyrna alone are rich in God's eyes for they possess a treasure which cannot be lost or pass away (cf. Mt. 6:19–21); every threat to this ownership, including that to their life itself by death, has already been changed for them by their risen Lord into a sure expectation of eternal life.

[10b]*Behold the devil is about to throw some of you into prison, that you may be tested, and for ten days you will have tribulation.*

For that reason, he can bluntly foretell a worsening of their situation without frightening them. The times and possibilities are measured by God for their persecutors whom the adversary of God himself uses as henchmen; they have only " ten days " at their disposal, a symbolic formula for a " short time."

[10c]*Be faithful unto death, and I will give you the crown of life.* [11]*He who has an ear, let him hear what the Spirit says to the churches. He who conquers shall not be hurt by the second death.*

In these words of encouragement the problem arises once more which earthly poverty and distress, human suffering as such poses for him who knows himself to be united to God in faith and who knows himself to be loved by him. A first, more factual, answer to this question was already given with the indication : " but you are rich "; it is here complemented from a subjective angle. Cross and suffering serve according to God's intentions as a test in which the believer is to prove his loyalty to him (the theme of the book of Job); in this way the believer wins the prize of victory in combat, similarly to a contestant in the arena (cf. Lk. 24:26; Rom. 8:17). " The crown of Smyrna," a sports distinction of that time, withers; as a combatant's prize for the victory of faith God has set up the crown of eternal life. Christ would like to be able to give the title " the faithful Smyrna " to his church there in another, eternal and forever valid sense; the consequence of this will be that he will be able to preserve its members from the " second death," the condemnation at the judgment (cf. 20:6. 14; 21:8).

Letter to the Church in Pergamum (2:12–17)

[12]*To the angel of the church in Pergamum write : the words of him who has the two-edged sword : . . .*

Pergamum, once the capital city of the Attalide kingdom, had rescued something for the present out of its great past, among them a stately library of 200,000 scrolls (according to Pliny); pergamena (writing material from specially prepared animal skins) bears its name from this city. It was overtopped by a specially magnificent acropolis with temples and palaces; on its slope stood the altar of Zeus (pergamum altar) already admired in antiquity. As early as 29 A.D. the city had a temple of Augustus and Roma and became the oldest place of the emperor cult in Asia Minor. The great pilgrim's shrine of Asklepios, the God of healing, possessed the greatest significance. The "throne of Satan" could have referred to one of the magnificent cultic buildings of Pergamum; however, in all likelihood, it alludes quite generally to the atmosphere of a city permeated by a heathen religiosity which as a milieu in which the Christians breathed and lived was also a temptation for them. A clear separation is here necessary; hence the Lord introduces himself to them as the bearer of the "sharp two-edged sword."

[13a]*. . . I know where you dwell, where Satan's throne is; . . .*

He knows the milieu ruled over by Satan in which the Christians of Pergamum live, the temptations and allurements which this implies bringing with it the danger of being amenable to syncretic interim solutions. Christ and Satan have nothing in common (cf. 2 Cor. 6:14), hence for Christians there is no compromise possible on this point, either theoretical or practical.

The one true God and his revelation can by nature never tolerate idols and false salvific doctrines.

[13b]*. . . you hold fast my name and you did not deny my faith even in the days of Antipas my witness, my faithful one, who was killed among you, where Satan dwells.*

Despite these surroundings and its dangers there were in Pergamum Christians of such clear decisiveness that they in conviction and deed, in true freedom of spirit and devotion of heart preserved their faith in Christ uncounterfeited and unbroken up to that point of sacrifice which Antipas had demonstrated in his death of witness to Christ. Loyalty to the faith is indeed almost the self-evident basic requirement of Christian life as such; yet the Lord knows that its fulfillment in the background of the concrete circumstances of a human life is no longer so self-evident; and therefore he expressly praises the community at Pergamum for it.

[14]*But I have a few things against you : you have some there who hold the teaching of Balaam, who taught Balak to put a stumbling block before the sons of Israel, that they might eat food sacrificed to idols and practice immorality.* [15]*So you also have some who hold the teaching of the Nicolaitans.* [16]*Repent then. If not, I will come to you soon and war against them with the sword of my mouth.*

To be sure not all emerged from the spiritual combat and practical seduction equally unsullied; a minority let themselves be infected by heathen practices and the theories which inspire them. Their condition and its danger is characterized by a comparative image from the history of the Old Testament people of God where there is talk of a worship of idols and fornication (Num.

25:1f.; 31:16; cf. also 2 Pet. 2:15; Jude 11). This minority
represent the same views as the Nicolaitans at Ephesus (cf. 2:6);
they thought they could make certain concessions to the spirit
of the times and the place which in their opinion were also possible to Christians, but in reality they amounted to a break with
Christian teaching and practice (cf. also 1 Cor. 6:12–20; 20:14–
22). Christ calls on those gone astray at Pergamum to repent;
otherwise he will have to take action himself with a clear
sentence of judgment on the counterfeitors of the true reality of
Christian life, make an end to the indecision of the community
in their regard. As in Pergamum, it is always a battle against
two fronts which Christianity in the world must endure, against
hostility and detraction from the outside and against dangers of
false doctrines from within.

*[17]He who has an ear, let him hear what the Spirit says to the
churches. To him who conquers I will give some of the hidden
manna, and I will give him a white stone, with a new name
written on the stone which no one knows except him who
receives it.*

The victor in this combat is promised the prize of victory with a
double metaphor. The manna had marvelously kept Israel alive
in the wilderness and brought them safely to the Promised Land.
If the manna is called here " hidden " manna, it could be an
echo of the idea developed by Jewish scribes in connection with
the tradition, recorded in 2 Macc. 2:4f., that Jeremiah hid the
Ark of the Covenant, and the manna preserved in it, before the
temple was destroyed: the food from heaven will be kept
hidden till the final time; in any case, a kind of food is meant
here which cannot be had till a future date, namely, the banquet
or marriage feast of eternal life (cf. Lk. 14:15–24; Mt. 22:1–14).
Since the letter has mentioned judgment twice (12:16), the

metaphor of the white stone is perhaps best explained by a peculiarity in the ancient process of justice, that the judges announced their verdict of not guilty by proffering a white stone; hence this metaphor would mean a declaration of innocence in the court of God. The image, however, receives the additional detail of a new name to be written on the stone, probably the new name of the one who receives the stone. Name meant no less than essence in ancient times; hence the victor will be joyfully aware of his very personal relationship with God which he alone will be able to experience (cf. 1 Jn. 3:1f.).

Letter to the Church in Thyatira (2:18–29)

[18a]*And to the angel of the church in Thyatira write: ...*

Thyatira, a smaller city in Lykustal, lived from commerce and trade; chief occupations were weaving and dyeing; the dealer in purple, Lydia came from Thyatira (Acts 16:14f.). Because of the zinc mines in the vicinity the ore-processing industry was also represented there. Comparable to the guilds, there were in such cities trade unions of the same group of craftsmen which as in the middle ages also had certain religious affiliations; the day of the patron god was solemnly celebrated by special sacrifices each year.

[18b]*The words of the Son of God, who has eyes like a flame of fire, and whose feet are like burnished bronze.* [19]*I know your works, your love and faith and service and patient endurance, and that your latter works exceed the first.*

Jesus introduces himself to the community with his highest title of majesty: in contrast with the frequency of this title in John's Gospel it is met only this once in Revelation. The two other titles come from the vocation-vision (1:14f.); the blazing majesty of his divine nature, the omniscience and omnipotence of the Lord sitting in judgment over the communities is expressed thereby. His aim is to appeal urgently to the conscience of the head of the community; to begin with, however, the good members receive a word of recognition, brief in its form but in content a very high praise. Their love and faithfulness are demonstrably genuine in their service for one another; to this is added their staunch endurance which had not weakened despite the difficulties which had arisen for the community from within and without. This recognition finds its climax in an assertion, contrasting with the judgment on the church at Ephesus (2:4), that in their Christian life clear progress is discernible since former times.

[20]*But I have this against you, that you tolerate the woman Jezebel, who calls herself a prophetess and is teaching and beguiling my servants to practice immorality and to eat food sacrificed to idols.*

This sharp criticism is directed against their tolerance and indulgence of false tendencies and erroneous trends as they had also appeared at Ephesus (2:6) and Pergamum (2:14f.). At Thyatira there stood at the head of these aspirations a woman who falsely claimed the charisma of prophecy for herself (cf. Acts 13:1; 21:9; 1 Cor. 12:28; Eph. 2:20; 4:11); she is called by a symbolic name, Jezebel, because her bad influence at Thyatira is like that of the Phoenician princess of the same name, whom King Achab took to wife and who abused her position by introducing into Israel the worship of her homeland idols and its immoral cults and led the king himself astray (3 Kings 16:21–34). With the allegedly spirit-inspired doctrine, which permitted the partaking of sacrificial meals and a certain moral laxness, that false prophetess made it possible for many in Thyatira to live with less friction among their work colleagues especially in the trade unions. An ironically meant citation from the propaganda vocabulary of her followers leads one to suppose that this trend was an early form of Gnosis. When they allegedly believe to have experienced the " deep things of Satan " (2:24), this must mean that they were convinced of his powerlessness; with this their deeper knowledge they justified the irrelevance of participation in sacrificial meals and their other libertine freedom catchwords (cf. 1 Cor. 8:1–7).

[21]I gave her time to repent, but she refuses to repent her immorality. [22]Behold, I will throw her on a sickbed, and those who commit adultery with her I will throw into great tribulation, unless they repent of their doings; [23]and I will strike her children dead. And all the churches shall know that I am he who searches mind and heart, and I will give to each of you as your works deserve.

The Lord took his time till he intervened, in order to give the erring ones time to come to themselves and repent. This time of grace has now expired because their stubbornness leaves no hope for improvement. With his intervention the Lord will start with the first offender; she will be struck down by an illness, surely one leading to her death as " her children " (v. 23), that is, her followers, are being punished by death. In case of a second group " those who commit adultery with her " the punishment is not so extreme; they must not be true followers but merely sympathizers with her false doctrines; reflection and repentance is in their case not yet out of question. The fate of the teachers of false doctrine in Thyatira is meant as a warning to all communities that their Lord will come on them with just judgment if they misunderstand his patience and do not use the time for repentance.

²⁴But to the rest of you in Thyatira, who do not hold this teaching, who have not learned what some call the deep things of Satan, to you I say, I do not lay upon you any other burden; ²⁵only hold fast what you have till I come.

The last exhortation is addressed to the faithful in Thyatira, to hold fast to the attitude they have shown till now; they will not be overburdened, the Lord assures them of this with words from the decision of the Apostolic Council (Acts 15:18); laxity he detests, but also rigorism is not in his nature; it is important that they preserve that which at the beginning he had singled out as praiseworthy.

²⁶He who conquers and who keeps my works until the end, I will give him power over the nations, ²⁷and he shall rule them with a rod of iron, as when earthen pots are broken into pieces, even as I myself have received power from my Father; ²⁸and I will give him the morning star. ²⁹He who has an ear, let him hear what the Spirit says to the churches.

The victor-text refers to the special situation of the church in Thyatira. Not concessions and adjustments to the non-Christian environment will establish them in the world; there are limits set by unadulterated truth and lines drawn by the holy will of God. He who keeps to them will at some future time share the authority of Christ over the world, after he has first—as promised by the images from Ps. 2:8—also shared in the judgment of Christ on a rebellious world (cf. 1 Cor. 6:2; Acts 19:14f.). The second promise is somewhat obscure but is clarified by Rev. 22:16, where Christ characterizes himself as the morning star; not only a participation in his power does he promise but himself too as a reward to the victor; he will share in the shining light, the glory of the transfigured Son of man. The demand to give heed to the words of the Spirit is from now on added to the victor-text in the letters.

Letter to the Church in Sardis (3:1–6)

[1a]And to the angel of the church in Sardis write: . . .

Sardis was the old royal town of the Lydians; the last king who resided there was Croesus who entered legend on account of his riches; there was not much left of their former greatness except the memory of a glorious past. Its citizens like those in Thyatira lived mainly from the wool-processing industry. Their historical decline down to their present unimpressive state is a symbol of what has become of the Christian community of late in Sardis.

[1b]The words of him who has the seven spirits of God and the seven stars. I know your works; you have the name of being alive, and you are dead.

The community has given up the ghost, it has died except for the few. Therefore Christ appears to them, as he did to the church at Ephesus, as Lord and protector of the " angels " (cf. 1 : 16) of the seven communities and as the " life-giving spirit " (1 Cor. 15 : 45) who embodies the fullness of the Spirit of God (cf. 1 : 4), of whose " fullness " the Church lives (cf. Jn. 1 : 16; Col. 2 : 9).

[2]Awake, and strengthen what remains and is on the point of death, for I have not found your works perfect in the sight of my God.

Without beginning, as he did so far in the letters, with a word of praise the Lord opens the argument with the church at Sardis with an extremely sharp rebuke. His lucid, impatient and harsh

judgment—underlined by the assertion that they would not endure in the sight of God—is meant to have a shock-effect to
shake the community out of their death-like sleep and bring them
back to their senses. Otherwise they will sleep on without notic-
ing how it is with them and where their condition will finally
lead them; they in fact exist only in name, that bit of reality
which is the church at Sardis exists only in a vanishing minority
with little signs of life; this remainder too will soon have died
if considerable help is not forthcoming.

*³Remember then what you received and heard; keep that and
repent. If you will not awake, I will come like a thief, and you
will not know at what hour I will come upon you.*

The call to awake from this deep sleep of death, from a sham
Christianity without life, a façade of only external Christian
observation which in reality is already a coffin-lid, sounds like a
loud military command. The following good advice to begin with
specifies as a means of revival to recall the wakeful receptivity
and the lively readiness of the first hours when Sardis heard the
gospel and the Church of Jesus Christ had taken root there; this
first enthusiasm must be recaptured, if the word of God is to
become fruitful in them once again and through them in their
environment. If the call to repentance should remain without
result then there will soon be a sudden and terrible awakening
for the Christians in Sardis when they will be confronted quite
unprepared with their unexpected judge (cf. Mt. 24:42); the
threat of judgment puts an exclamation mark of warning behind
the serious exhortation.

*⁴Yet you have still a few names in Sardis, people who have not
soiled their garments; and they shall walk with me in white,
for they are worthy.*

As always and everywhere for the Church in the world, for Sardis, too, not everything is lost; among so many dead some are still alive, who have proved themselves faithful and their works perfect in the sight of God despite the bad spirit of the whole group with their sluggish indifference, their spiritless habituations, their sleepy indolence. Those who " have not soiled their clothing," that is to say, those who have not betrayed their newly given existence in Christ and its corresponding external expression in doing and not-doing will in time to come share in the glory of their transfigured Lord (" in white "). The illusionary and fleeting impression which we make on people here is immaterial but what does matter is how we appear in the sight of God for all eternity.

[5]*He who conquers shall be clad thus in white garments, and I will not blot his name out of the book of life; I will confess his name before my Father and before his angels. He who has an ear let him hear what the Spirit says to the churches.*

The first image of the victor-text is linked to the local industry of wool-processing, as already in the description of the good in Sardis. Pure, gleaming white is in Revelation the color of transfiguration in God's heaven and of those who find a place there. The second image uses the idea of the " book of life," the list of the citizens of heaven, which can be found in the Old Testament (e.g. Ps. 69[68] : 29) and in the New Testament (Lk.10:20) and especially frequently in Revelation (13:8; 17:8; 20:12; 21:27). The third image repeats the promise of Jesus in the gospel (Mt. 10:32; Lk. 12:8) where he personally guarantees the eternal salvation of those who did not avoid the discomfort of confessing him even against the spirit of their " worldly " environment.

Letter to the Church in Philadelphia (3:7–13)

7aAnd to the angel of the church in Philadelphia write : . . .

A Lydian small town which about eight years before suffered terribly from an earthquake, Philadelphia remained since then small and insignificant compared with its neighboring cities. Thus her Christian community was not large; moreover, it was under attack from outside but excellent in spirit and order. Like the Christians in Smyrna, the Lord expresses his unlimited praise for them. As in Smyrna, the distress seems to have been caused by the hostility of the Jews. The main concern of the letter is to arouse confidence, to strengthen the manifest loyalty and to inspire courage for the future.

7bThe words of the holy one, the true one, who has the key of David, who opens and no one shall shut, who shuts and no one opens.

Christ introduces himself here with epithets which are not taken from the vocation-vision. In the fifth seal-vision (6: 10) of the martyrs God is called " holy and true "; in these two predicates Jesus reveals his divine essence and with the third he testifies to his Messiahship; a verse from Is. 22:22 which prophesies that Eliacim would receive the office of being in charge of the royal palace is here interpreted Messianically and the house of David is made a symbol of the Messianic kingdom. Jesus alone decides who is accepted into the kingdom of God of the final time, or who remains excluded.

8I know your works. Behold I have set before you an open door, which no one is able to shut; I know that you have but little power, and yet you have kept my word and have not denied my name. ⁹Behold, I will make those of the synagogue of Satan who say that they are Jews and are not, but lie—behold, I will make them come and bow down before your feet, and learn that I have loved you.

The small band of Christians from Philadelphia, who numerically in the midst of the total population hardly count, did not let this position make them insecure or intimidate them; on the contrary, they have applied the strength of their living faith openly for missionary purposes. That which, perhaps despite their efforts, they did not achieve is promised them by him who makes successful all human missionary possibilities by his grace: the community will receive new members and, indeed, from the ranks of their declared and most stubborn opponents. He will convince these that now the Christians are the true " Israel of God " whom he has lovingly adopted in his Son. The prophetic promise of the homage of heathens to Israel (cf. Is. 45 : 14; 49 : 23; 60 : 14) will now also be fulfilled in that the first chosen people, who has lost its election through its own fault, will show this honor to the new people of the new Covenant of God.

¹⁰*Because you have kept my word of patient endurance, I will keep you from the hour of trial which is coming on the whole world, to try those who dwell upon the earth. ¹¹I am coming soon; hold fast what you have, so that no one may seize your crown.*

Besides this visible success whereby the Lord wishes to reward their unsullied fidelity he will show his appreciation by still another deed; as he opens the door for the Jews to them, he will shut them to the powers of persecution; he will see to it that in the coming general persecution of Christians they will stand the test and will suffer no losses through apostasy. If the time of tribulation is, however, short, then the Lord will come and fetch them to their eternal reward; as in a sporting contest the crown of victory demands that one does not stop in the middle of the course but keeps running to the winning post.

[12]*He who conquers, I will make him a pillar in the temple of my God; never shall he go out of it, and I will write on him the name of my God, and the name of the city of my God, the new Jerusalem which comes down from my God out of heaven, and my own new name.* [13]*He who has an ear, let him hear what the spirit says to the churches.*

Letter to the Church in Laodicea (3:14-22)

[14a]*And to the angel of the church in Laodicea write : . . .*

Laodicea in Phrygia, situated on the Lykos, had developed into a rich commercial and industrial center since its foundation about four hundred years before. Linen and wool-weaving were the main branches; the bank institutions of the city had a good reputation as far as Rome itself (Cicero); there was also a medical and pharmaceutical school there. After the earthquake of the year 60 A.D. the city completed the work of reconstruction from its own resources without state aid. In this last letter the local peculiarities are used especially fully for the composition of images.

[14b]*. . . The words of the Amen, the faithful and true witness, the beginning of God's creation.*

The church at Laodicea is the only one in whose favor not a single word is said; it is a community which had also caused the apostle Paul no little anxiety (Col. 2:1), he had also written a letter to them (Col. 4:16) and a few decades after Christ's criticism the community collapsed completely through religious tepidity due to a false *rapprochement* with the world. And yet even for them the Lord has not merely words of judgment; at the end of the letter we find like in no other of the seven letters the most heartfelt words of appealing love.

Christ introduces himself with the personified Hebrew affirmative particle, " Amen " (cf. Is. 65:16), which is then explained by the " faithful and true witness " (cf. 1:5), his word is absolutely dependable. He is also the prime source of the entire creation (cf. Jn. 1:3) to whom therefore all created things remain always linked (Col. 1:16); hence if they are seeking the world, the Christians of Laodicea find in him the only correct approach to it, and to the world itself in its most original form.

[15]*I know your works : you are neither hot nor cold. Would that you were cold or hot! *[16]*So, because you are lukewarm, and neither cold nor hot, I will spew you out of my mouth.*

The false " not only but also " with which they attempt to compromise between being a Christian and being worldly makes them abhorrent to their master like a drink of lukewarm water; one is tempted to spit it out. Nothing half, nothing whole, a limping on two sides (cf. 3 Kings 18:21), not against God, not against the world (cf. Mt. 6:24; 12:30), in this way one gets on with everyone all the time; yet such an indecisive Christianity is in Christ's judgment more tasteless than genuine paganism, a Christian without character has less worth in his eyes than a pagan of strong character. Truth and faithfulness are of his essence; he who wishes to belong to him must imitate him in this respect.

[17]For you say, I am rich, I have prospered, and I need nothing; not knowing that you are wretched, pitiable, poor, blind, and naked.

The Christians of Laodicea are rich in earthly goods, from the outside too the community presents a fine picture, externally they want for nothing; they can fulfill and do all needs and duties, especially also those of a charitable nature. Socially they get on well with others because they have achieved an integration with the world; but precisely for that reason the Christians of this city are neither a vexation nor a witness (cf. Mt. 5:13). Because blinded they no longer see this duty they have to the world, self-deluded as they are they come to the conclusion that they are putting up a good show not only before men but also before God. With such conceited self-righteousness the Lord deals harshly in his tribunal of justice; with five adjectives he makes clear the wretched condition of his church at Laodicea.

[18]Therefore I counsel you to buy from me gold refined by fire, that you may be rich, and white garments to clothe you and to keep the shame of your nakedness from being seen, and salve to anoint your eyes, that you may see.

The Lord does here for Laodicea what he once told about the shepherd who went after the one lost sheep till he found it (Lk. 15:4); he offers to help. They can obtain the genuine gold from him which retains its value in heaven as well (cf. Mt. 6:20) and which already on earth alleviates poverty before God; only clothed with the righteousness which grace confers (cf. 1:17) will they stand properly before God, and the grace of Christ will also give them the adequate vision for a true self-understanding. Further it is noteworthy here that the Lord offers his grace; the freedom of him who accepts or rejects is preserved.

The three images whereby the Lord illustrates and offers his necessary help are moreover closely connected with the local realities of banks, weaving and the medical-pharmaceutical institute.

[19]*Those whom I love, I reprove and chasten; so be zealous and repent.* [20]*Behold, I stand at the door and knock; if any one hears my voice and opens the door, I will come into him and eat with him, and he with me.*

In the letter to Laodicea words of appealing love follow the call to repent. In case of such self-assured and self-righteous people the appeal of love is more likely to be successful than a demanding order. Hence the Lord begs like one standing outside before a locked door to be once more let into Laodicea, after he had first excused the harsh strictness with which he had to deal with them as a special expression of his love; for an indulgent and compliant love never helped anyone; God, in any case, chastises and disciplines when he loves. The meal which the Lord intends to have when he gains entrance once more will put a new seal on the betrayed friendship.

[21]*He who conquers, I will grant him to sit with me on my throne, as I myself conquered and sat down with my Father on his throne.* [22]*He who has an ear, let him hear what the Spirit says to the churches.*

With the allusion that Jesus himself had to fight for his glory and sovereignty on the throne of his Father (Lk. 24:25), the victor-text promises a share in the sovereignty of God over the universe in the consummated kingdom of God to those who do not surrender to the world but overcome it (cf. 1 Jn. 5:4) by his example (Jn. 16:33) with the strength of their faith.

PART II:

The Prophecy of the Future of the Church up to the Final Consummation
(4:1—22:5)

INTRODUCTION: THE SOVEREIGN LORD AND TRANSFER OF POWER TO THE LAMB
(4:1—5:14)

Before the prophetic description and interpretation of the final time the foundation is laid in a preparatory vision for a proper understanding of the mighty images which depict the course of the world towards its end. A look into heaven discloses to the Seer the invisible background, the guiding force and the decisive might of world history. Although externally history might appear as a self-contained chain of human decisions, as a linked series of human actions and omissions, this external view does not give a complete picture; for history is through and through determined by the decisions of God himself. The creator and sovereign is not indifferent to, and detached from the evolution of his handiwork; rather he himself acts in history with man and, if necessary, against man to bring his creation towards the goal set for it. Indeed, with the incarnation of his Son, he himself has passed into the history of his world in an unheard-of manner and with this happening he has posited the real and finally decisive deed of history. After the Son of God had subjected himself to the order of the transitoriness of all creatures and had taken on himself the lot of man till death, he, then, with his resurrection outstripped the provisionality of this transitory being for everyone and for all things and in his transfigured form he has announced the future eternal form of God's creation. Raised to the right hand of the Father, the Crucified has thus become the destiny of the world and, therefore, has been appointed by the Father as Lord and guide of its history.

The preliminary vision 4:1—5:14 depicts this reality in glowing images which in many details are reminiscent of the portrayal of the visionary experiences of Old Testament prophets (Is. 6:1f.; Ezek. 1:3) but in their execution they are throughout independently realized. In order somehow to describe the mystery and the world of God, illustrative material from this-worldly experience alone stands as the prophet's command; he uses this material as a simile in order to impart a mediate, analogical and, therefore, unsatisfactory yet, in its way, a true representation of God's reality.

The reproduction of a vision in words can, moreover, be distinguished from the experience itself; that it sometimes can become difficult to embody a visionary experience in words can be deduced from the explanation of the apostle Paul (2 Cor. 12:1-4). This circumstance must also be taken into account for the subsequent writing down whereby John recorded his visions; it is therefore comprehensible that in the presentation he uses images known to him from the Old Testament and from the Jewish apocalyptic writings.

The Vision of God's Throne Room (4:1-11)

¹After this I looked, and lo, in heaven an open door! And the first voice, which I had heard speaking to me like a trumpet, said, Come up hither, and I will show you what must take place after this. ²ªAt once I was in the Spirit, . . .

The same angelic voice, which had called him before the vocation-vision (1:10), announces to John that he is to be shown the future evolution of world history as it is determined (" must ") in God's plan and the destiny of the Church of Jesus Christ within it. Immediately the new vision sets in, which he experiences in an ecstasy linked with an experience of rapture. In the dome of heaven, which according to ancient belief stretches over the earth's disc in the form of a half-sphere, John sees an open door which he approaches at the command of the angel. In those days one believed God's heaven to be above the firmament; hence John knew what the angel wanted to show him.

[2b]. . . and lo, a throne stood in heaven, with one seated on the throne! [3]And he who sat there appeared like jasper and cornelian, and round the throne was a rainbow that looked like an emerald.

He sees the region of God like a throne room in which the throne itself and the one sitting on it immediately catch the eye; the name of God is not uttered out of reverence as it was the custom among the Jews; for his essence is anyhow unutterable. This throne and he who sits on it is not only the central point of heaven, it is also the center of the whole world and its history; here is the fullness of all sovereignty in heaven and on earth. Not dead laws and blind fate, but the will of him who sits on this throne determines everything that shall be. The appearance of the throne and the one on it is not described by the Seer, " he dwells in unapproachable light which shines on the entire surroundings. The " glory of the Lord " which he endeavors to describe is a central concept of the Bible; it means the absolute majesty, power and perfection of the divine essence, which radiates from him like an unearthly glow of light and makes him unapproachable (cf. Ex. 24:16f.; 33:18–23; 40:34; 3 Kings 8:10f.; Is. 6:1f.; Eph. 1:17; 1 Jn. 1:5).

The sparkling glory in light of the divine majesty is compared with colors of gleaming and flaming precious stones; their names do not coincide with those of today; thus jasper probably refers to that white diamond which breaks light up into all colors, or to the opal which is also iridescent; and the cornelian is probably the red ruby. Like a canopy the rainbow (cf. Ezek. 1:28) stretches over the throne and radiates a light-green light (emerald). If the wreath of light, which does not emit the natural colors of the rainbow, is nevertheless called a rainbow then this sign of peace between God and mankind would indicate here that God uses his power as grace; he is a merciful Lord who "plans for welfare and not for evil" in order to "give hope" (Jer. 29:11). All evil in history does not have its source in him but he uses it for his court of justice.

The entire picture emits an infinite calm; the absolute power of God does not need a support from outside, nor all the unrest and disturbing means, including war, which on earth are connected with the establishment and securing of power. In times of insecurity and upheaval man looks more radically for that which can truly guarantee his existence; the concept of God which these apocalyptic images impart can truly pacify anyone who is able to believe that the glorious, omnipotent and merciful God absolutely and without doubt brings about the welfare of the world even though the path to this goal on account of the perversity of man goes through catastrophe which can serve the wicked as well as the good as a trial for their welfare.

⁴Round the throne were twenty-four thrones, and seated on the thrones were twenty-four elders, clad in white garments, with golden crowns upon their heads. ⁵ᵃFrom the throne issue flashes of lightning, and voices and peals of thunder, . . .

Who God is and what comprises his sphere of sovereignty is in the vision then mediately clarified by the royal household and the liturgy which they perform before the throne. The twenty-four elders make the outer full-circle around the throne; their thrones, their golden crowns and white garments are reminiscent of the victor-texts (3:21; 2:11; 3:5); hence they are humans who have won the prize set up for the victors. The number twenty-four, twelve and twelve, is probably best interpreted with reference to the old and new Covenant (twelve tribes, twelve apostles) whose unity is made quite clear in the image of the apocalyptic woman (12:1–17); the number twenty-four could also be linked to the twenty-four priestly castes of Israel (Chron. 24:4–5. 7–18), the more so as the elders performed liturgical functions (4:10f.). They are obviously conceived as representatives of the entire people of God which in its already transfigured members represents the Church in adoration before the throne of its sovereign Lord. Lightning and peals of thunder which go out from the throne are reminiscent of the revelation of God on Sinai (Ex. 19:16–19) and indicate that this so seemingly unapproachable and transcendent God is, at the same time, the God of Sinai, that is, of salvation history; this reminder of the revelation of the God of the Covenant and of its conclusion fits in well with the interpretation of the elders.

[5b]. . . *and before the throne burn seven torches of fire, which are the seven spirits of God;* [6a]*and before the throne there is as it were a sea of glass, like crystal.*

Between the elders and the throne burn seven torches which were mentioned already in the greeting (1:4), they are expressly interpreted as symbols of the Holy Spirit (cf. also Mt. 3:11; Acts 2:3 for symbolic relationship between fire and spirit). Not till later is something said about the floor of the heavenly throne room; this detail, we presume, is to give besides the impression of infinity that of calm clarity—in contrast with the chaotic primeval waters and its remainder, the oceans of the world—and the light-flashing celestial brilliance of this heavenly ocean.

[6b]*And round the throne, on each side of the throne, are four*

living creatures, full of eyes in front and behind : [7]*the first living creature like a lion, the second living creature like an ox, the third living creature with the face of a man, and the fourth living creature like a flying eagle.* [8]*And the four living creatures, each of them with six wings, are full of eyes all round and within, and day and night they never cease to sing, Holy, holy, holy, is the Lord God Almighty, who was and is and is to come!* [9]*And whenever the living creatures give glory and honor and thanks to him who is seated on the throne, who lives for ever and ever,* [10]*the twenty-four elders fall down before him who is seated on the throne and worship him for ever and ever; they cast their crowns before the throne, singing,* [11]*Worthy art thou, our Lord and God, to receive glory and honor and power, for thou didst create all things, and by thy will they existed and were created.*

Quite near the throne, John sees a final group of four creatures who are evidently standing on the four sides of the throne conceived as detached; their prototypes are in Ezekiel (1:5-14) and Isaiah (6:2-4); yet here they do not appear, as in Ezekiel, as the bearers of the throne but as the nearest throne attendants; moreover John has broken up the four-faced monstrous form which they have in Ezekiel and has given each a separate, distinctive appearance; the many eyes also come from Ezekiel 1:18 (on the wheels of God's chariot) and 10:12 (the cherub), the six wings and the trisagion from Isaiah 6:2f.

Four is in Revelation the cosmic number (four points of the compass), in addition the fact that the creatures are compared with four earthly creatures, the strongest of their type, highlights the fact that these represent creation before the throne of their creator just as the elders represent redeemed mankind. The multiplicity of eyes symbolize their rapture, admiration and astonishment at the sight of God and their large number of wings symbolize how quickly they are ready to fulfill the will of the sovereign Lord. Hence they represent the ideal image of God's creation in its paradisical originality and therefore they also fulfill the highest task of all creatures to praise without a pause the glory of the creator. Three times their cry resounds, three names are given to God, threefold is the praise they offer the triune God as the creator and sovereign of the universe; truly a cosmic liturgy, which the ideal picture of the Church at the throne of God in the form of the twenty-four elders makes completely its own; as a sign that as those saved they also owe existence, salvation and transfiguration to God alone they lay their golden crown before the throne. The "Worthy art thou," with which the solemn acclamation at the entry processions of the Roman emperor began when he had himself honored as a manifestation of divinity, is only intended for him who can claim unlimited power over all things because to him alone as the creator of the universe belongs everything.

The Vision of the Transfer of Power to the Lamb
(5:1-14)

[1]*And I saw in the tight hand of him who was seated on the throne a scroll written within and on the back, sealed with seven seals; . . .*

The second part of the vision brings movement into the lofty, almost too unapproachable picture of the heavenly throne room with its liturgy performed respectfully and in a measured manner. This image remains there like a background; but in front of it an action of such great significance unfolds that attention is drawn to it by moments of tension expressly set before it. As to content this section illustrates with a gripping image the article of faith: " ascended into heaven, where he is seated on the right hand of the Father." The One on the throne holds his right hand with a scroll stretched forward in a proffering gesture. The piece of writing is a so-called episthograph, that is, the outside and the inside of the rolled-up parchment or papyrus strip are written on, a sign of the fullness of content (cf. Ezek. 2:9f.). For the purpose of keeping secret what is in the scroll it is sealed with seven seals (as in 1:1 seven is a symbol of wholeness). The book which contains world history in its entire evolution as God's salvation history is the property of the sovereign Lord; but he intends giving it to someone else. Everything in the picture now evolves around this scroll and him who is receiving it and will be made known and at the same time realized by him who receives it.

[2]*And I saw a strong angel proclaiming with a loud voice, Who is worthy to open the scroll and break its seals?* [3]*And no one in heaven or on earth or under the earth was able to open the scroll or to look into it,* [4]*and I wept much that no one was found worthy to open the scroll or to look into it.* [5]*Then one of the elders said to me, Weep not; lo, the Lion of the tribe of Judah, the root of David, has conquered, so that he can open the scroll and its seven seals.*

The tension is brought on by a literary device also used in the Old Testament, that of rhetorical questions (cf. 3 Kings 22:19–21; Is. 6:8). Moreover, in this way it is heavily stressed that the task in question here absolutely transcends all creatures of God; no angel, no man, no devil is able to look into the secret plan of God, even less to realize it. No science, no ever so lofty an ethos, no ever so perfect a commitment of the best will bring the world to its goal. This knowledge, which indeed is not merely an objective reality, but also concerns man in his own existence, makes the Seer very sad; an experience of such absolute impotence only knows the outlet of tears. These tears, however, have another special cause in the context of the whole; John would have to know something of the content if he is to console effectively and encourage in loyalty the distressed Church. Then one of those who represent the Church in its state of perfection takes on his cause, one of those witnesses who already know God as he is because their faith has already been transformed into vision. He discloses to John that in reality there is one, indeed, a human being, who is able and worthy to accept God's offer, the Messiah of God, whose sovereign power and strength was already foretold in the Old Testament in two Messianic epithets (Gen. 49:9; Is. 11:1), and as man he has "conquered" in the history of the world by one unique act and thereby has identified himself as the one to whom "full authority has been given in heaven and on earth" (Mt. 28:18).

6And between the throne and the four living creatures and among the elders, I saw a Lamb standing, as though it had been slain, with seven horns and with seven eyes, which are the seven spirits of God sent out into all the earth; 7and he went and took the scroll from the right hand of him who was seated on the throne.

And already John sees the victor in the circle of the heavenly court standing immediately before the throne. Introduced as a "lion," he appears as a "Lamb" with the marks of slaughter. It can hardly be expressed more briefly and aptly when and how the victory, just referred to, was won; like a "lamb," the favored sacrificial animal of the old Covenant, this "lion" has given himself as an expiatory sacrifice for the sins of all (cf. 1:5); Revelation therefore especially likes the title "lamb" for the Redeemer (twenty-eight times; cf. also John 1:29). He has, however, demonstrated the strength of the "lion" by rising to eternal life (cf. 1:18) so that his name is simply the "living one" (1:18). Only as a sign of victory does the Lamb still wear the healed marks of slaughter; in addition it has "seven horns," a symbol of its unlimited power (horn is a symbol of strength; cf., e.g., Deut. 33:17; 1 Sam. 2:1.10; Jer. 48:25; Lk. 1:69); and its "seven eyes" symbolize the Spirit of God which belongs to him and is sent by him and works with full authority over all the world (cf. Jn. 15:26; 16:7–15). This "Lamb" therefore is able and worthy to have transferred on him the execution of God's decrees for the world and humanity. "The Lamb went up and took the scroll . . ." describes the ascent of the Lamb to the throne whereby the sovereign Lord hands to him the power he himself possesses. The destiny of all and for all therefore lies till the end in the hands of Jesus who has said of himself: "I have compassion on the crowd" (Mk. 8:1), in whom that heart, which he once permitted to be pierced for the love of mankind (cf. 1:7), continues to beat. This means for all who as Christians experience, or also suffer, the history of this world between the ascension and the return of the Lord a confidence of supra-human security and absolute certainty.

And when he had taken the scroll, the four living creatures and the twenty-four elders fell down before the Lamb, each holding a harp, and with golden bowls full of incense, which are the prayers of the saints; . . .

Already after the previous image the vision was explained in conclusion in a hymn; as generally in Revelation the same thing is happening here in such a hymn of praise; it is a hymn to God, to the Redeemer, in three parts. The first strophe is sung by the circle nearest the throne, the four creatures; the twenty-four elders also adopt it; in that way the two groups together perform the same homage to God (cf. 4:9f.). This description is based on the idea of the temple cult in Jerusalem; while the priests offered incense, the Levites, accompanied by string instruments, sang psalms (cf. 33[32]:2; 71[70]:22). Just as in the temple the rising cloud of incense was regarded as a symbol of the prayers of the entire people so in this text the ceremony is also interpreted as the "prayers of the saints," that is, the entire Church; the interpretation of the elders as representatives of the Church at the throne of God (cf. 4:4) also gains new support in this conception; they stand in a priestly role of mediator, representing the entire redeemed people of God.

[9] *. . . and they sang a new song, saying, Worthy art thou to take the scroll and to open its seals, for thou wast slain and by thy blood didst ransom men for God from every tribe and tongue and people and nation,* [10]*and hast made them a kingdom and priests to our God and they shall reign on earth.*

The "new song" as it was composed and sung in the old Covenant for the occasion that Israel had experienced a new, great deed of God (cf. Ps. 96[95]:1; 149:1; Is. 42:10), takes up the question of the angel regarding who is worthy (5:2) and supplies the answer. It glorifies Christ, the Saviour of the world, who through his death achieved a liberation from the slavery of the powers of evil and has formed the redeemed from all nations (four members!) into a holy community of God, to whom they have access like the priests in Jerusalem at the temple services, who even lets them share in his sovereign power (cf. 1:6); all this has become reality for the redeemed with the ascent of the Lamb to the throne, for which reason they sing their "new song." Moreover, the circumstance that precisely the four creatures, the representatives of the cosmos, intone the song underlines strongly the cosmic significance beyond mankind of the redemptive act of Christ (cf. Rom. 8:20–23).

[11]Then I looked, and I heard around the throne and the living creatures and the elders the voice of many angels, numbering myriads of myriads and thousands of thousands, [12]saying with a loud voice, Worthy is the Lamb who was slain, to receive power and wealth and wisdom and might and honor and glory and blessing! [13]And I heard every creature in heaven and on earth and under the earth and in the sea, and all therein, saying, To him who sits upon the throne and to the Lamb be blessing and honor and glory and might for ever and ever! [14]And the four living creatures said, Amen! and the elders fell down and worshipped.

The countless hosts of angels join into the song of praise of the throne attendants, also the entire earthly creation in its great manifoldness without exception takes it up; the four creatures say the Amen and the elders conclude this truly cosmic liturgy with the cult of worship. Hence the entire picture presents a prophetic vision of the consummation which is the goal of the turbulent evolution which is about to be described after this introduction. In such a profound vision all riddles of history are solved, just as the suffering and death of Jesus become first transparent and sensible in the vision of the Lamb's ascent to the throne.

THE VISIONS OF THE SEALS (6:1—8:1)

The introductory vision (4:1—5:14), which is put at the head of the first series of plagues but serves as such for all which follow, was to fix the standpoint from which the symbolic portraits of future development are to be contemplated if they are to be correctly understood. Presupposing the right orientation, the insight emerges: besides God there are no independent forces which make history; all powers and figures which appear in history, and who seem to determine it by their own power, are in fact subject to God's disposition, and that of his Anointed, who, seated at the right hand of the Father, with full authority guides and brings to its good end the realization of God's plan for the world as a redemptive plan for his creation.

Essentially and fundamentally only God makes history, because he holds securely in his hand even the contradictions and catastrophes which are caused by other forces which are in themselves free but are also circumscribed by the absolute freedom of God; he fixes their limits as to time and place and is able to consign even to this chaos and confusion a positive sense and purpose. The meaning of the catastrophic epochs in the course of history is revealed by keeping in mind the final judgment on all the deeds and omissions of mankind, and especially on the phenomena of evil forces, of which they are a prognostic; their purpose consists in clearing the impediments out of the path of the unfolding of God's kingdom, which God's adversaries either directly or indirectly seek to set up against it, and thereby to work towards its final consummation.

In order to avoid possible misinterpretations of the plague

visions one must not forget that all descriptions in Revelation are symbolic images, which means that they do not predict future events as they might occur concretely sometime in the future. In order to understand, especially the seal visions, one must also take note that not only the scroll and the seals together represent a symbol but also each individual seal is assigned with a symbolic meaning. One thing to remember generally about apocalyptic images is that only to a lesser degree can they be compared with a naturalistic portrayal of reality—be they portrayed statically (slide) or in movement (film)—as with dream images which in their progress can unfold in such a way that their first content is completely exchanged for another at the end.

Strictly speaking one could not look into the first part of the scroll till all the seals have been opened; the latter, however, would mean that the entire plan of God for his world would be disclosed; but disclosed, as the following shows, means in the focus of Revelation the same as fulfilled, that is to say, to be completely disclosed would mean that the course of history has come to an end. If, however, contrary to a technically correct conception, a course is already set in motion with the opening of each seal this then indicates that we are dealing with preparatory events, which indeed are aimed at the fulfillment of God's final Will, the consummated kingdom of God, but they do not by themselves already realize this kingdom step by step. Even the synoptic apocalypse (Mt. 24:4-44) draws similar sketches of catastrophes and adds the explanation: " all this is but the beginning of sufferings " (Mt. 24:8; Mk. 13:8). This guide to interpretation is valid for all three series of plagues of John's Revelation (seals-trumpets-bowl plagues) which rise out of one another and like a spiral with ever-increasing force rush towards the central point, the second coming of the Lord; like labor pangs before birth they foretell the Lord's coming and prepare for it.

The First Four Seals (6:1-8)

¹Now I saw when the Lamb opened one of the seven seals, and I heard one of the four living creatures say, as with a voice of thunder, Come! ²And I saw, and behold, a white horse, and its rider had a bow; and a crown was given to him, and he went out conquering and to conquer.

The first four seals form a close unity having the same motif, namely, the "four apocalyptic riders " (A. Dürer); their task, indicated by various colors and equipment, also represents a unity in itself. The concise and strikingly etched images take their elements from the nocturnal visions of the prophet Zechariah (1:8-10; 6:1-8) but with their aid they are executed as independent projects. The background to this course of events remains the image unfolded in the introductory vision. The Lamb opens one seal after the other. The course of events, which is triggered off by it, is each time set in motion by one of the four creatures (representative of the cosmos) with a cry of command like thunder; no disaster comes from God, rather from the sphere of created forces; the almighty power of God and the Lamb is in this picture revealed by a majestic silence.

The rider on the white horse reminds one at first sight of the Logos rider (19:11-13); like the latter he appears as a conquerer; the crown which is given him symbolizes, as is expressly added in words, the invincible victor; the prototype of this image could have been the riders equipped with bows known from the Persian offensive troops which were never completely conquered by the Romans.

Christ himself could hardly be recognized in this image since he is already represented in the image of the Lamb opening the seals; moreover, he could never appear at the command of a creature (one of the living creatures). Nor could the victorious course of the gospel through the world, which according to Mark must have been accomplished before the end of time, come in to play here as a possible interpretation. If one of the riders differed from the other three in not being regarded as a bringer of calamity, then the group of riders undoubtedly produced and conceived as a closed unity would be dissolved. In Mt. 24:6 the first named as one of the tribulations of the final time is war; this is probably what the first rider means. There is the possibility, however, that the image of the leading rider concurs with the most important figure of the final happening: the antichrist, under whose successful rule chaos is nearing its end. This idea comes readily to mind for two reasons: in the synoptic apocalypse right at the beginning, immediately before the prediction of war, there is the warning against false pretenders to Messiahship; besides, the white color and the victor's crown would fit in with this picture since the antichrist is throughout Revelation presented as an attempt to ape Christ (cf. 13:1–9) and will be victorious in the final time till the returning Lord dethrones him (cf. 19:11–21).

In this first image, which shows forces hostile to God and antagonistic to creation at work, one meets for the first time the stereotype formula, "he was given," which recurs in similar descriptions. This passive form would have God as a logical subject; this passive paraphrase had developed in Judaism in order not to have to call God by name. With this formula, John constantly reminds us that despite the sometimes obtrusive outward impression no manifestation or effect of the power of evil is autonomous, that it can only be at work because, and as long as, God permits it.

[3]And when he opened the second seal, I heard the second living creature say, Come! [4]And out came another horse, bright red;

its rider was permitted to take peace from the earth, so that men
should slay one another; and he was given a great sword.

The second rider is by his marks clearly recognizable as a bringer
of calamity. Red, the color of blood and fire, is in Revelation the
mark of powers hostile to God (cf. 12:3; 17:3; 17:4). His
instrument is the sword and his work is war and, indeed, it
would seem that the words " slay one another " refer rather to
civil war (cf. Mt. 24:7) which compared with wars between
nations—symbolized by the first rider—usually take on a more
gruesome and devastating aspect; to this extent the effects of the
second evil power seems an aggravation of the first. Wars with
other states and wars within the state (rebellion and violent
upheaval) both have their driving power from evil; hence no
type of bloody conflict can ever be rendered harmless by a
euphemism like " holy war " or even by providing with the
adjective " religious."

[5]*When he opened the third seal, I heard the third living creature*
say, Come! And I saw, and behold, a black horse, and its rider
had a balance in his hand; [6]*and I heard what seemed to be a*
voice in the midst of the four living creatures saying, A quart
of wheat for a denarius, and three quarts of barley for a
denarius; but do not harm oil and wine!

The third rider on the black horse comes almost always after the
first and second, after war; he symbolizes famine (cf. Mt. 24:7)
and its effects are widespread death (the black color). The scale
on which the rations are weighed drastically depicts the shortage
of food and the information concerning the price of the most
important type of bread grain refers to the rising prices. A
denarius was in those days a day's wages. The damage done by
the rider of calamity is confined to the spring harvest; the fruits

of the autumn oil and wine are expressly omitted. The possibilities of destruction which this third rider possesses are expressly limited by a higher power which he must obey.

7When he opened the fourth seal, I heard the voice of the fourth living creature say, Come! 8And I saw, and behold, a pale horse, and its rider's name was Death, and Hades followed him; and they were given power over a fourth of the earth, to kill with sword and with famine and with pestilence and by wild beasts of the earth.

The fourth rider on a sickly pale (color of a corpse) horse is called by name. Of course, the Greek word *thanatos* can besides death also mean pestilence or epidemic disease in general; probably the latter meaning is intended here; for death accompanies every rider being his intrinsic terror; that the end of v. 8 is taken directly from Ezekiel where we read (Ezek. 14:21) ". . . my four sore acts of judgment: sword, famine, wild beasts and pestilence " is a clue to the validity of the wider meaning. Just as the third rider the fourth also has his fixed limits which he may not transgress.

The terrifying aspect of the last rider is aggravated further by his retinue, Hades; like a beast of prey it awaits its victim which falls to it in the wake of the rider. The vision of the four bringers of calamity ends thus in one image which is like the late medieval sketches of the " dance of death."

Moreover, the apocalyptic riders in this vision are not regarded as harbingers of the imminent end of the world, just as little as the text parallel in meaning of the synoptic apocalypse, " the beginning of sufferings " is regarded as a sign of the approaching end. In the whole of the time between the ascension and the second coming of the Lord, in the final time, these devastating powers and forces exercise their work of destruction in history.

It is significant that they appear at the command of a created being and not that of God. Earthly perversity, political and economic desire for power, hate and envy born of need or pride again and again enter the scheme of things. Not God but the world itself impedes paradise on earth. Even if the faithful are drawn by all this evil into suffering with the rest they will know, however, that God is master of all epochs and all that happens in them; this certainty assures them that all afflictions are intended by God as visitations for their good (cf. Rom. 8:28).

The Fifth Seal (6:9–11)

⁹*When he opened the fifth seal, I saw under the altar the souls of those that had been slain for the word of God and for the witness they had borne; . . .*

With the breaking of the fifth seal the throne room of the Almighty is changed into a celestial temple with an altar, a replica of the altar of burnt-offering at Jerusalem, at the base of which the blood of the slain animals was poured out as a sign that their life had been offered to God. John therefore sees the Christian martyrs at the foot of the heavenly altar because they are offerings who have been slain for God's word and for the witness they had borne (cf. 1:9). In the synoptic apocalypse the description of the " beginning of sufferings " (cf. the vision of the riders) is also followed by the prophecy of severe persecutions (Mt. 24:9). Just as the " faithful and true witness " (3:14) completed his total surrender to the Father on the cross, so the victims of persecution have given up their lives for God through the grace of their Master's sacrifice and in imitation of his mind and loyalty. Hence they are now like the Lamb in the sanctuary of heaven near to God.

[10] . . . they cried out with a loud voice, O sovereign Lord, holy and true, how long before thou wilt judge and avenge our blood on those who dwell upon the earth? [11]Then they were each given a white robe and told to rest a little longer, until the number of their fellow servants and their brethren should be complete, who were to be killed as they themselves had been.

With a loud cry of prayer they become advocates before God for their persecuted brothers on earth. In them, the Church, the Church of martyrs, maltreated and tortured by " those who dwell on earth "—a standing expression in the Revelation for the ungodly—calls to the sovereign Lord, whose nature is holiness and truthfulness, that salvation from the injustice and wickedness of this world might soon be accomplished by the revelation of his glory before all the world; this cry of prayer basically requests the same thing as the cry of longing with which Revelation closes: " Come, Lord Jesus! " (22:20). The prayers of the martyrs, which they offer to God mindful of the sufferings of their brothers on earth, do not express a need for reprisals from a thirst for vengeance, rather a hunger for righteousness and the victory of truth, for the completion of God's kingdom (" thy kingdom come! ").

To their question: " How long? " they receive a twofold answer. The first which concerns themselves, is realized in a symbolic action, the conferring of a white robe, that is to say, they themselves already receive a share in the glory of the victor at God's throne (cf. 3:4f.). After that they are told, regarding the need of their brothers, that the number of martyrs determined beforehand is not yet complete; the plan of eternal wisdom, justice and goodness must first be followed to the end, then the moment will have come which the Church with its martyrs hopes and longs for. The martyrdom of the faithful helps to complete the Church and hence hastens the hour of the world's consummation. As long as it exists on earth, it is of the Church's essence that her continued existence is put into question. As a whole, she knows herself to be neither dependent on the favor of the world, nor mortally threatened by the world's rejection; like the psalmist she staunchly professes her confidence in the sovereign Lord: " my times are in thy hand " (Ps. 31 [30] : 16; Lk. 18:5f.).

The Sixth Seal (6:12–17)

[12]*When he opened the sixth seal, I looked, and behold, there was a great earthquake; and the sun became black as sackcloth, and the full moon became like blood,* [13]*and the stars of the sky fell to the earth as the fig tree sheds its winter fruit when shaken by a gale;* [14]*the sky vanished like a scroll that is rolled up, and every mountain and island was removed from its place.*

The misfortunes of the first five seal visions were caused by human beings, hence they remained confined to men and their world; in the sixth seal vision the misfortune spills over into inanimate nature and at once takes on cosmic dimensions. In the synoptic apocalypse too we find that such cosmic catastrophe immediately precedes the final judgment of the world (Mt. 24: 29) which one would expect with the breaking of the seventh seal. As an introduction to the " day of the Lamb's wrath " Revelation produces a horrifying, gripping image which is totally put together from Old Testament motifs; on the threshold of her last day the earth begins to quake, the sun too is extinguished as if it had put on a black garb of mourning, the bright sky has become black (cf. Is. 50:3), on this dark background the full-moon hangs blood-red (cf. Joel 3:4); the entire universe seems about to dissolve, the stars fall from their firm position like the fall of figs from the defoliated figtree when the winter storms buffet it (cf Is. 34:4). This symphony of downfall, which has been created with the ideas concerning the universe prevalent at that time and is also to be interpreted symbolically, ends with the disappearance of the entire sky-consistency, which is imagined as spreading in a half-sphere over the earth; like a scroll the firmament is rolled up (cf. Is. 34:4). The chaos on earth is also of such proportion that its surface is no longer recognizable; even the mountains symbols of permanence and the islands are no longer found in their old place. The dissolution of all order in the human life-space confronts mankind with the chaos of the end and lets it also foresee its own destruction.

[15]*Then the kings of the earth and the great men and the generals and the rich and the strong, and everyone, slave and free, hid in the caves and among the rocks of the mountains,* [16]*calling to the mountains and rocks, Fall on us and hide us from the face of him who is seated on the throne, and from the wrath of the Lamb;* [17]*for the great day of their wrath has come, and who can stand before it?*

The panic which grips mankind when it sees its world tear at the seams and break into pieces, grips all without exception; seven groups (symbol of completeness) are listed, from the highest social caste to the lowest class of society. The feeling of impotence in the face of nature, whose laws man has discovered and thereby regards them to a certain extent under his control, drives men to the depths of despair; all pride has crumbled under a hopeless fear. They try to escape but there is no hiding place for their bad conscience and from the eyes of the Lamb appearing in judgment; the day of his wrath will reveal that the redeemer of the world is also the judge.

The seal visions clear away the utopian idea that an external progress in man also signifies progress in humanity, that, so to speak, automatically a humanizing process runs parallel with it. On the contrary, the images of the breaking of seals reveal the maturative process of evil in history and the growth of chaos and anarchy which corresponds to it. In the end the dissolution of the order of nature shows frightened mankind what he himself has done by rejecting the order entrusted to him; he has thereby undermined his own existence. What now confronts him in his world is the frightening emptiness of nothingness which means only destruction and end without any escape. The immeasurable existential anxiety, which grips all, is impressively portrayed by the flight—and hiding—psychosis; in the total instability of man in his world, which he believed to have made his own and bent to his service, the consciousness of moral responsibility once more dawns on him, but only in the form of a fear of judgment.

One generation of humanity will be the last; what this generation will actually experience is here proclaimed only in symbolic images; how the reality will look, we do not know; the aim of the apocalyptic portrayal is to illustrate dramatically the inner condition and the reaction of those last people faced with God's final judgment. In conclusion, the cataclysms in history and nature, of which the seal visions tell, are interpreted to mean that thereby the "wrath of the Lamb," his day of judgment, is proclaimed.

The First Interlude (7:1–17)

The course of the eschatological process seems to have moved quite close to the end with the breaking of the sixth seal. At this moment of highest tension an interlude interrupts it which in a double vision answers the question for the faithful which was put at the end of the sixth seal vision by the ungodly: " who can stand? " (6:17). The forlornness and despair of " those who dwell on the earth " is set up against the preservation and hopeful expectancy of the faithful as a contrasting piece. The motif of encouragement and consolation, which runs like a red thread through the whole structure of Revelation, is here enuciated with special vigor in the midst of an atmosphere of destruction (cf. also Lk. 21 : 28).

To the question: How will it stand with the elect in this time of collapse? the answer comes: with God's special protection they will not perish on earth and will be guided through the turbulent transience of this world to their goal before the throne of God. In two closely linked images: the Church in the midst of the chaotic world-time and the same Church in the light and peace of eternity with God these promises are highlighted.

The Elect on Earth (7 : 1–8)

¹*After this I saw four angels standing at the four corners of the earth, holding back the four winds of the earth, that no wind might blow on earth or sea or against any tree.* ²*Then I saw another angel ascend from the rising of the sun, with the seal of the living God, and he called with a loud voice to the four angels who had been given power to harm earth and sea,* ³*saying, Do not harm the earth or the sea or the trees, till we have sealed the servants of our Lord upon their foreheads.*

Four angels contain the forces of annihilation, which like whirl-winds are to complete the ravaging of the earth (cf. Jer. 49 : 36; Dan. 7 : 2f.), at the four corners of the earth like bloodhounds on a chain. World-time has always been a story full of storms; these increase the nearer the end approaches. But something special happens to the Church before it is wrapped and buffeted in, and with the world by these storms. An angel appears— promising good already by the fact that he appears from the sunrise, the east where the Jews judged the paradise of the final time would be; he carries the seal of God in his hand with which he is to mark the elect before the beginning of new tribulations. In ancient times, animals and slaves were branded as the property of their master; also the members of specific cults had themselves branded by the mark of their god (e.g., the followers of Dionysius, an ivy leaf). Moreover, what John describes here has its prototype in Ezekiel (Ezek. 9:2–7); the prophet sees how the God-fearing inhabitants of Jerusalem are marked with the letter Tau on the forehead by an angel so that they should be saved from the judgment which God intends to mete out to the apostate city. To have a seal set on the forehead therefore means belonging and a promise of protection. With this symbolic action God does not promise his own that they would be saved from the storms, but kept safe in the storms and while they last (cf. Jn. 17:15).

And I heard the number of the sealed, a hundred and forty-four thousand sealed, out of every tribe of the sons of Israel, ⁵twelve thousand of the tribe of Judah, twelve thousand of the tribe of Reuben, twelve thousand of the tribe of Gad, ⁶twelve thousand of the tribe of Asher, twelve thousand of the tribe of Naphtali, twelve thousand of the tribe of Manasseh, ⁷twelve thousand of the tribe of Simeon, twelve thousand of the tribe of Levi, twelve thousand of the tribe of Issachar, ⁸twelve thousand of the tribe of Zebulun, twelve thousand of the tribe of Joseph, twelve thousand sealed out of the tribe of Benjamin.

The symbolic number of those who received the seal is given as 144,000 (12 × 12 × 1,000); the product of the square of the number of completion, twelve, and the number of a crowd, thousand, conveys that the number of elect is complete and that they amount to a great multitude. The receivers of the seal are evenly distributed over the twelve tribes of the Old Testament people of the Covenant, for God is no respecter of persons. Judah, as the Messianic tribe stands first; Dan is missing but instead Manasseh, the son of Joseph is inserted. The naming of the twelve tribes must also be understood symbolically here (cf. Jas. 1:1); in the new people of God there is no longer any difference between Jews and heathen (cf. Rom. 10:12; Eph. 2:11–22); "Israel according to the flesh" (1 Cor. 10:18) no longer plays a special part in the new "Israel of God" (Gal. 6:16), which is equally composed of Jews and heathens; so in the vision of the complete city of God in heaven the names of the twelve tribes are also inscribed on the gates (21:12), and the names of the twelve apostles on the foundation-stones of its walls (21:14).

The Elect in Heaven (7:9–17)

[9]*After this I looked, and behold, a great multitude which no man could number, from every nation, from all tribes and peoples and tongues, standing before the throne and before the Lamb, clothed in white robes, with palm branches in their hands,* [10]*and crying out with a loud voice, Salvation belongs to our God, who sits upon the throne, and to the Lamb!* [11]*And all the angels stood around the throne and round the elders and the four living creatures, and they fell on their faces before the throne and worshipped God,* [12]*saying, Amen! Blessing and glory and wisdom and thanksgiving and honor and power and might be to our God for ever and ever! Amen.*

A second vision, in which John is shown the same multitude having arrived at its goal, follows the first of the elect on earth.

Not so much for the completeness of the theme as for pastoral reasons is the vision of the consumation already faded in at this stage which from the point of view of the subject matter should not appear until the section 21:1—22:5. This vision is a necessary complement to the first in so far as the promised deliverance in the first is presented as realized in it in its fullest and final measure. Only with this completion is the intention of the interlude to awaken the conviction of security and the courage to confess the faith, if need be, even to the extent of surrendering one's life, fully realized.

The symbolism of 144,000 is here right at the start translated into reality when it is said that the multitude of the elect from every nation is innumerable and stand transfigured ("clothed in white robes") at the throne of God after they had victoriously (palm as a symbol of victory), with God's help and under his protection, battled through all the ordeals of the earth; the combatants are at their goal as victors. Their hymn of praise contains the joyous recognition that they owe their salvation and happiness to God and the Lamb who have proved themselves faithful to their promises. All the angels of heaven and the two groups of throne assistants confirm this in a similar liturgy and with almost the same words as in 5:12; there the praise was addressed to the Lamb, here it is meant for God, the last source of all salvation. They allowed no force on earth to constrain them, before God alone does redeemed mankind bend the knee in deep gratitude.

¹³*Then one of the elders addressed me, saying, Who are these, clothed in white robes, and whence have they come?* ¹⁴*I said to him, Sir, you know. And he said to me, These are they who have come out of the great tribulation; they have washed their robes and made them white in the blood of the Lamb.*

The hortative purpose of the twofold vision is then made expressly prominent in a special scene by a twofold question. One of the elders asks the Seer who they are that he sees transfigured at the throne, and how they arrived there. Gripped with emotion and awe (" Sir "), John does not dare to answer the question; so the elder who knows better than anyone on earth can now explain what John sees. He is looking at the innumerable multitude of those " who have come out of the great tribulation," that is to say, they have endured the controversies and trials of the final time with God's help (being among the " number of the sealed ") in such a manner that they could be awarded the robe of victory (cf. 3:5). Their achievement was not first and foremost their own desert; the way to transfiguration had first to be opened for them by the expiatory death of the Lamb who accomplished forgiveness and readmission into God's company; but it is their personal deed inasmuch as they corresponded with the promptings of God's grace and accepted God's offer of salvation; both facts are concisely expressed in an image, produced with reference to the symbolism and hence somewhat contradictory in its outcome, namely, that of washing white in the blood of the Lamb.

[15]*Therefore are they before the throne of God, and serve him day and night within his temple; and he who sits upon the throne will shelter them with his presence.* [16]*They shall hunger no more, neither thirst any more; the sun shall not strike them, nor any scorching heat.* [17]*For the Lamb in the midst of the throne will be their shepherd, and he will guide them to springs of living water; and God will wipe away every tear from their eyes.*

Glory and happiness before the throne of God is founded (" therefore," v. 15) on the grace of redemption on the one hand,

and on the other on the free acceptance of, and cooperation with God's offer of salvation; the latter they have proved by their faithful, patient endurance of tribulation and persecution on earth. Hence they deserve to live once more like the first man in paradise with God and be before him without interruption, forever (" day and night "). In God's society they have also been freed of every kind of earthly anxiety, distress and need; they live in God, hence live in his happiness (" God will shelter them with his presence," v. 15). Their service before him is no longer the fulfillment of a duty, but the joyful recognition of the creature who now at last has found himself completely in his creator and experiences in his love the fulfillment beyond all expectation of desires till now unfulfilled. In conclusion, and therefore especially stressed, the Lamb is named as the mediator of this happiness; with the image of the good shepherd, the Lord himself had in the past illustrated his concern for his own (Jn. 10: 1–18); the promise he added to this self-portrait was : " I give them eternal life and they shall never perish " (Jn. 10: 27f.). This promise he has made to come true, he has guided them to the pastoral land of eternal happiness and to the springs of eternal life.

With the second image the interlude has fully realized its intentions; the assurance of God in the first image : I will see you through! was meant to awaken courage and confidence, the description of the glorious goal in the second image is meant to impart decisiveness and enthusiasm in taking on the unavoidable combat for it. So after this glimpse of eternity, we are again called back into the hard reality of time; in it our eternity is decided; therefore our earthly existence is in no way devalued by this hope, on the contrary, it has given it an importance which could neither have been discovered, nor established in it without it.

The Seventh Seal (8:1)

[1]When the Lamb opened the seventh seal, there was silence in heaven for about half an hour.

With the breaking of the seventh seal the last impediment is removed and the contents of the scroll can be scrutinized and made known. The silence of even the heavenly choirs for a while (half an hour = short while) impressively depicts the tension with which all await the final conclusion of the divine plan of salvation. Yet the contents of the seventh seal contain more than the end of time which contrary to expectation has not yet arrived. Such patient waiting as God requires of the faithful can at times be a hard trial while the unbelievers take it as an encouragement. Out of the last seal there unfolds once more a group of seven plagues which are portrayed in the trumpet visions; compared with the first series of plagues ("beginning of sufferings") they imply an aggravation. The nearer the end, the more intense and clearer the visitations because the need for conversion becomes more urgent.

THE TRUMPET-VISIONS (8:2—11:19)

Introduction (8:2–6)

²Then I saw the seven angels who stand before God, and seven trumpets were given to them.

Just as in the seal-visions the occurrences in history and nature were made dependent on a happening in heaven, so the introduction to the trumpet visions leads one to understand that the supernatural and the natural are not in themselves closed domains shut off from one another, rather that nothing occurs on earth which was not prepared and determined in heaven. The unity of heaven and earth is found in God who neither deserted his world nor left it to itself after he created it. For this reason the trumpet visions are also introduced by a liturgical procedure in the heavenly temple which is once more described in imitation of the liturgical rites in the temple at Jerusalem. There the priests, assigned to the offering of incense, carried the glowing coals in a golden bowl from the altar of burnt-offerings to the altar of incense and then sprinkled the incense on them. During the offertory ceremony the priests gave the people outside the sign for worship with trumpet blasts.

In the celestial liturgy the angels take the place of the priests: thus " the seven angels who stand before God " (cf. Tob. 12:15) are given these wind instruments. Like orderlies, always prepared for a command and therefore imagined as standing in the immediate vicinity of the throne, these seven highest spirit creatures are also called in the Jewish apocalyptic literature " angels of the countenance " and " angels of the presence " or

81

simply " archangels." The trumpet is the instrument with which, according to Scriptures, especially the eschatological events are announced (Mt. 24:31; 1 Cor. 15:52; 1 Thess. 4:16). Just as in the first four seal-visions the plagues set in at the command of a creature " with a voice like thunder " now it occurs each time at the blast of a trumpet which the seven angels produce in turn.

³And another angel came and stood at the altar with a golden censor; and he was given much incense to mingle with the prayers of all the saints upon the golden altar before the throne; ⁴and the smoke of the incense rose with the prayers of the saints from the hand of the angel before God.

Still during the half-hour silence in heaven, and before the seven angels gave their signals, " another angel " moves towards the heavenly altar which was already referred to in 6:9 and is now conceived as an altar of incense to offer the incense on it. The rising smoke of the incense is once again, as in 5:8, linked with the " prayers of all the saints " (cf. Tob. 12:12; Ps. 141[140]:2); the angels of heaven adopt as their own the prayers of those marked by God's seal and bring them purified before God's face. The blessed spirits in heaven pray with the distressed Church on earth; she ought therefore never feel forsaken, rather she should always feel secure.

⁵Then the angel took the censor and filled it with fire from the altar and threw it on the earth; and there were peals of thunder, loud noises, flashes of lightning, and an earthquake.

In an abrupt transition the image of security and peace is followed by one of horror and judgment. The angel fills the censor with the glowing coal from the altar on which the prayers of " the saints," that is, the faithful on earth, rise up, and throws it

down upon the earth. An explicit explanation of this symbolic
action is not found in the text but it is hinted at in the results
recorded. Thunder, lightning and earthquakes announce God's
judgment (Ezek. 10:2) on those who seek to assert their in-
dependence outside the order of God and against his salvific will.
This second act of heavenly liturgy, the announcement of judgment, is causally connected with the first, the adoration and
petition before the divine majesty; " the saints," who have been
appointed priests and co-rulers with God through the redemptive
act of the Lamb (5:8–10), become partners through their prayers
in the fate of the world.

*6Now the seven angels who held the seven trumpets made ready
to blow them.*

That the threatened judgment will begin soon is announced by
the fact that the angels prepare to blow; yet they must wait for
the moment which God alone determines.

The First Four Trumpets (8:7–12)

Like the seal-visions this second group of seven is also sub-
divided; in each case a complete unity is formed by the first four.
The four trumpet-plagues do not directly strike mankind like
the corresponding seal-plagues but they affect his living-space; the
order of nature goes out of joint. Similar natural cataclysms
already occurred with the breaking of the sixth seal; there they
served to announce the approaching judgment, here, on the
contrary, they are independent plagues and judgments of God
(cf. Lk. 21:24f.). Despite all of their horror, that these occurrences do not yet mean the end is indicated by the curtailment

of their destructive power to a third of each stricken area. Certain Old Testament presentations are without doubt recognizable as prototypes of the descriptions of individual catastrophes, such as the Egyptian plagues and the destruction of Sodom; once again an indication that the apocalyptic events are not meant literally but symbolically. Also the succession of plagues should be understood as a planned order not as a temporal succession. Gigantic forces are released in the natural sphere for the work of destruction; if the apocalyptic images seem less fantastic to us nowadays, rather remind us of certain feared modern weapons of destruction, it should help us to grasp the images better; however it must not be forgotten that these images do not deal with real but with symbolic descriptions in which certain essential characteristics of what is coming in the future are disclosed but not its concrete configuration.

⁷The first angel blew his trumpet, and there followed hail and fire, mixed with blood, which fell on the earth; and a third of the earth was burned up, a third of the trees were burned up, and all green grass was burned up.

The first trumpet announces misfortune for the earth. The time for clemency had passed which had earlier on (7:2) been proclaimed for all on the earth. Field, wood and meadows are struck remorselessly; the seventh Egyptian plague (Ex. 9:23) also records such tempestuous weather. Aggravating the description of the Egyptian plague, the writer of Revelation adds the rain of blood (cf. Joel 3:3f.). This conception probably had its source originally in the natural phenomena, observable in the Far East, that swirled up desert sand sometimes colors the rain red; this manifestation was looked upon as a bad omen. Man and beast are struck as well by the devastation of the ground and the plant growth since their nutritional possibilities are curtailed; the loss of a third of the produce is a lot and is felt generally.

8The second angel blew his trumpet, and something like a great mountain, burning with fire, was thrown into the sea; 9and a third of the sea became blood, a third of the living creatures in the sea died, and a third of the ships were destroyed.

With the second trumpet signal the sea was struck by disaster, portrayed imaginatively by the fall of a fiery great mass, as big as a mountain. In what measure and how clearly the apocalyptic images owe their origin to the imagination, and how little to realistic phenomena is once more highlighted here; it is not the effects of heat and mechanical force which seem to kill the water creatures rather than the change of the water into blood as it is stated in imitation of the first Egyptian plague (Ex. 7:20f.); the foundering of a third of the ships is comprehensible through the rising sea. Perhaps these apocalyptic images, which grow like dream-images, are consciously kept somewhat at a distance from natural experience in order to indicate that it is not the natural event but the sign into which God makes it that is the important factor.

10The third angel blew his trumpet, and a great star fell from heaven, blazing like a torch, and it fell on a third of the rivers and on the fountains of water. 11The name of the star is Wormwood. A third of the waters become wormwood, and many men died of the water, because it was made bitter.

At the third blast of trumpet something extraordinarily horrifying happens: a great star, flaming like a meteor entering the atmosphere, falls from the sky; a sign that God is behind the occurrence. John then perhaps sees this ball of fire exploding and spraying its poisonous contents over a third of the fresh water. Consequently the drinking water is poisoned; hence the star is named after the wormwood plant which, because of its strong bitter taste, was thought to be poisonous in ancient times (cf. Jer. 9:15; Amos 6:12).

¹²*The fourth angel blew his trumpet, and a third of the sun was struck, and a third of the moon, and a third of the stars, so that a third of the light was darkened; a third of the day was kept from shining, and likewise a third of the night.*

The fourth trumpet curtails the possibilities of life on earth still further; light, without which nothing grows and flourishes, is reduced by a third. The ninth Egyptian plague (Ex. 10:21-23) is here apocalyptically drafted out. The universe's sources of light are reduced by a third of their light-capacity, that is, a partial eclipse of the stars is announced (cf. Mt. 24:29); it is remarkable that in addition they lose a third of their shining time, once more a sign that the images are drawn expressionistically, more from the aspect of their significance.

The limitation put on these judgments of God characterizes them as threats and harbingers of God's judgment to come and as a call to repentance; the time for grace and the possibility of conversion are still at hand.

Intermediary Image: The Woes of the Eagle (8:13)

¹³*Then I looked, and I heard an eagle crying with a loud voice, as it flew in midheaven, Woe, woe, woe to those who dwell on earth, at the blast of the other trumpets which the three angels are about to blow!*

Before the three outstanding plagues set in, which in contrast
with the ones so far no longer merely strike the life-space of
mankind but man himself directly, they are expressly announced
by a triple cry of woe which uncannily echoes from the zenith
over the entire earth. They are the loud cries of an eagle which
also in other places of apocalyptic literature functions as God's
messenger of doom; flying high up in heaven he is visible to all.
His calls of woe are meant for " those who dwell on earth,"
that is, the ungodly (cf. 3:10) who subsequently are especially
singled out by the following catastrophes.

The Fifth Trumpet; The First Woe (9:1–12)

[1]*And the fifth angel blew his trumpet, and I saw a star fallen
from heaven to earth, and he was given the key of the shaft of
the bottomless pit;* [2]*he opened the shaft of the bottomless pit, and
from the shaft rose smoke like the smoke of a great furnace, and
the sun and the air were darkened with the smoke from the
shaft.*

The natural cataclysms of the first trumpet-plagues already trans-
cended natural possibilities in extent and effect; the plagues
which follow now appear on the whole as being outside the
sphere of nature; they do not come out of the atmosphere or the
cosmic space spread out above it, but from below, out of the
domain of demons. With them, those powers appear for whom
the No to God and his world has become the quintessence of
their existence and an expression of their perverse nature; lies,
contradiction and hate exercised with a boundless anger determine their activity; hence the threefold woe over the world
and mankind, before creation is left to the mercy of these terrible,
destructive forces. But here too, right at the start, we find the

" divine passive ": " he was given " (cf. 6: 1f.; also 20: 1–3. 7) as a sign that these forces cannot appear and work independently but are permitted to do so by God in order to bring men to their senses.

" A star fallen "—in apocalyptic literature a symbol for a fallen angel (cf. 12:9; Lk. 10:18)—that is to say, an apostate and damned angel, expressed figuratively in language which betrays the world-view of that age, receives the authority to let hell loose on mankind. The smoke from the dark pit of fire, in which the unhappy creatures are held captive (cf. Jud. 6:2; Pet. 2:4), now spreads its infernal darkness over mankind.

³*Then from the smoke came locusts on earth, and they were given power like the power of scorpions of the earth; ⁴they were told not to harm the grass of the earth or any green growth or any tree, but only those of mankind who have not the seal of God upon their foreheads; . . .*

The transference of the allegorical image is set down in the text itself when the demonic figures appear out of the smoke; the condition and behavior of hell spreads over the earth after the vision of heaven is cut off by the black smoke of Hades and the light of God can no longer shine for man; the " eclipse of God " is the consequence of that obscuration which God's adversary brings with him whither he goes. The image itself borrows some of its features from the eight Egyptian plagues (Ex. 10:14f.), the description of a locust attack in the prophet Joel (Joel 1 and 2), and the destruction of Sodom (Gen. 19:28). These creatures are compared with locusts to illustrate their vast quantity which darkens the sky as the dense swarms of these insects do; in their harmfulness they are more like scorpions than locusts; not the green of nature, but man is the object of their onslaught. Strange, and at first sight nonsensical, seems the circumstance that this plague strikes only the ungodly, that is, those people to whom the spiritually related hell should, if it is still possible, be well-disposed rather than hostile; yet one consequence of damnation is also self-laceration. But hell has no power over the " sealed " (cf. 7 : 2–8) who stand by God; they are expressly out of hell's range.

[5] *. . . they were allowed to torture them for five months, but not to kill them, and their torture was like the torture of a scorpion, when it stings a man.* [6] *And in those days men will seek death and will not find it; they will long to die and death will fly from them.*

The exclusion of the elect, and the command not to kill the ungodly are indications how their torment is to be interpreted; the bodily tortures are simply used as a drastic motif to portray allegorically their spiritual torment of those who abandon themselves to God's adversary by shutting themselves off from God. The symbolic content of this image is especially compact. He who is injected with the poison of hell becomes subject to a nameless torture and is in the end incarnate torment itself. Self-consuming doubt, fear of life, hopeless spiritual confusion, the cold atmosphere without love (cf. Mt. 24 : 12), the feeling of being homeless on earth and of being lost in the face of nothingness—all of this wears one down internally and leads to a despair which finally seeks death to find rest (Job 3 : 21f.).

The restrictions on the first four trumpet-plagues were merely spatial, with the fifth it is threefold : according to time (five months = a long time), according to scale (only the ungodly), according to manner (not to kill); as with the phrase " they were allowed," these oft-repeated restrictions recall to mind the sovereignty of God beside whom no other power can stand independently.

7In appearance the locusts were like horses arrayed in battle; on their heads were what looked like crowns of gold; their faces were like human faces, 8their hair like woman's hair, and their teeth like lion's teeth; 9they had scales like iron breastplates, and the noise of their wings was like the noise of many chariots with horses rushing into battle. 10They have tails like scorpions, and stings, and their power of hurting men for five months lies in their tails. 11They have as king over them the angel of the bottomless pit; his name in Hebrew is Abaddon, and in Greek he is called Apollyon. 12The first woe has passed; behold, two woes are still to come.

After the demon spirits had been described first as to their nature and operation, the description of their appearance is then filled in to clarify still further their demonic character. These are monstrous mongrel figures; they have something in common with locusts, war-horses, lions, scorpions, birds, indeed, even with human beings. Merciless severity (iron breastplates), passion of the furies (woman's hair, lion's teeth), an iron-hard ruthlessness (war-horses drawing chariots), deceitful force (scorpion's sting), subtly conceived torture (human faces), irresistible might (" crowns of gold " = emblem of victory), all this the description wishes to convey in order to represent with urgency the entire sinister nature of the diabolical will to destroy.

Where these gruesome forms come from, what they are and what their intention is, is in conclusion summarized in the naming of their leader; their king and commander is " the angel of the bottomless pit." To characterize his nature two names are given him; the Hebrew " Abaddon " = abyss, underworld (Job 26 : 6; Ps. 88 [87] : 12), is already in the pre-Christian Greek translation of the so-called Septuagint (LXX) rendered as " Apollyon "; origin and intention correspond, nature and appearance typify destruction.

With the fifth trumpet vision, the first woe, the power of hell has for the first time directly entered history after being active in earlier catastrophes as wire-puller behind the scenes. In the two woes still to come hell remains equally directly engaged and with increased ferocity. The time of the open pit and the smoke rising from it which darkens the sky and the face of God will continue.

The Sixth Trumpet; The Second Woe (9:13-21)

¹³Then the sixth angel blew his trumpet, and I heard a voice from the four horns of the golden altar before God,

The sixth plague is externally very like the fifth, that is to say, the demonic assaults continue but increase in scale and force. This time it is especially emphasized that God's will and salvific intention are behind everything that happens, also behind this chastisement at the end of time, even though it is executed by his adversary.

An auditory experience opens this vision (cf. 1:10); the voice comes from the golden altar of incense on which an angel, in the introductory vision to the trumpet-plagues (8:3f.), had offered the prayers of the saints together with the incense. This heavenly altar (which stands " before God ") has the same shape as the altars in the temple at Jerusalem; the four corners of the altar of burnt-offering as well as the altar of incense were curved upwards (into " horns "). The voice which comes down from the cover-plate of the altar evidently represents the answer to the prayers of the faithful on earth which the angel had offered to God. One could then infer from the content of the plague, which like the previous one strikes only the ungodly, what the contents of those prayers were; consequently the severely tried Christians of the final time would have prayed for alleviation and protection in their persecution by the ungodly.

[14]. . . *saying to the sixth angel who had the trumpet, Release the four angels who are bound at the great river Euphrates.* [15]*So the four angels were released, who had been held ready for the hour, the day, the month, and the year to kill a third of mankind.* [16]*The number of the troops of cavalry was twice ten thousand times ten thousand; I heard their number.*

The voice gives the angel, who has given the sixth trumpet-signal, the command to release four angels, fettered till then—their fetters indicate that they are angels of harm. The time of the release is fourfold determined (the cosmic number of completion); in God's world there are no independent forces of destruction; that the angels of harm are four in number also shows that the whole earth is at their disposal to kill a third of mankind. For this purpose they go as leaders at the head of the innumerable troops of cavalry with whose aid they will execute the devastation. The land at the Euphrates was in the Old Testament the seat of invasion into Palestine and the chosen people, so that finally the city of Babylon became in Israel a proverbial symbol of hostility to God. At the time of Revelation this river was the hot frontier of the Roman empire behind which the Parthians lay who with their feared troops of cavalry constantly harassed the eastern frontier of Rome and who were never finally defeated by the Roman legions. So with the naming of this locality the malevolent character of this image is still further underlined.

[17]*And this is how I saw the horses in my vision; the riders wore breastplates the color of fire and of sapphire and of sulphur, and the heads of the horses were like lions' heads, and fire and sulphur and smoke issued from their mouths.* [18]*By these three plagues a third of mankind was killed, by the fire and the smoke and the sulphur issuing from their mouths.* [19]*For the power of*

the horses is in their mouths and in their tails; their tails are like serpents, with heads, and by means of them they wound.

Already the humanly impossible number—literally: two hundred million—indicates super-human troops; the description of the horse and rider specifies them without doubt as demonic. Their hellish origin is made abundantly clear by the color of the breast-plates which are those of the infernal elements: fire, smoke and sulphur as well as the fact that they expectorate precisely these elements as means of destruction (cf. Job 41:11–13). John expressly emphasizes that his description should be regarded as only an attempt to put into words a visionary image ("in my vision") whose inner content but not external form has prophetic significance. Moreover, the image is not equally etched out in detail as was the case with the fifth trumpet. Among the weapons of the malfeasant riders their tails again receive attention as did those of the "locusts" (9:10), which are of a welter of serpents whose bite is deadly. With brutal force and uncanny treachery the lion-headed monsters attempt to destroy what crosses their path till the pre-determined quantity (one third) has been reached.

[20]*The rest of mankind, who were not killed by these plagues, did not repent of the works of their hands nor give up worshipping demons and idols of gold and silver and bronze and stone and wood, which cannot either see or hear or walk;* [21]*nor did they repent of their murders or their sorceries or their immorality or their thefts.*

The sinister image ends with the depressing realization: all means of heaven and hell which God sets in motion to bring the rebels to their senses come to nothing. His judgments are the last possibilities of divine love; but even with them he achieves nothing against willful imperviousness. Recent history also confirms the experience: the good get better through trials but the bad get worse. The demons, who have free access to the world, hasten thus the maturing process of evil. Genuine repentance, on the contrary, and this is part of the message of all the images, could change world history. Expansively and vividly John points out on what it finally depends when man in spite of everything does not come back to God and so to himself again; for the preservation of the idea of God also preserves the likeness of God. The "works of their hands," the world as men have made it, the great thing before which they stand in admiration, which they worship and from which alone they promise themselves help. Man in our technical civilization is at every turn, on quite a unique scale, confronted with his own achievements; he is proud of them and does homage to himself in his works and to his creative possibilities.

Man is thus God-forsaken and thrown back on himself; such spiritual perversity then produces also much moral disorder and aberration; belief and morality correspond as do unbelief and immorality (cf. Rom. 1:23–32).

The Second Interlude (10:1—11:14)

The trumpet-visions showed how God, in conflict with the maturing evil in the world of men, militantly advances his plan of salvation. His judgments become more frequent, more severe and more comprehensive; to the mass defection there corresponds a mass destruction initiated by the infernal spirits of contradiction against God and his order, propelled by hate of the creator and all his works. Injustice and upheaval, lovelessness and violence rule the world in which men now must live, and disgusted with their lives they despair. Thus far matters have progressed after the sixth trumpet, men no longer wish to live, the world is ready for the end which one expects will come with the seventh trumpet.

Yet, as after the sixth seal-vision, the course of events is now interrupted by an intermediary vision which like the one of chapter 7 aims to raise the courage and confidence of the faithful after the previous startling images, and to strengthen them for the expected worsening of the disasters.

The Angel with the Little Open Scroll (10:1-11)

¹Then I saw another mighty angel coming down from heaven, wrapped in a cloud, with a rainbow over his head, and his face was like the sun, and his legs like pillars of fire. ²He had a little scroll open in his hand, ³ᵃand called out with a loud voice, like a lion roaring; . . .

This section records a second calling of John; the place of this second vocation-vision is the same as the first (1:9), the place of banishment, Patmos. There appears an angel much out of proportion in shape; John sees him from Patmos standing with legs apart, one foot on the mainland and the other on the sea; his stature reaches high over the clouds which cover his body like a garment; his face, being near the sun, is bathed in its brilliance. Moreover, the whole apparition is decked out with the symbols which the transfigured Son of man was provided with in the vocation-vision (1:13ff.), or, like the rainbow, taken even from the vision of the One on the throne (4:3); such reflection of the glory of heaven identifies the angel as an ambassador of God and the Lamb; his appearance mirrors the sovereignty as well as the mercy (" rainbow ") of God.

Yet the overpowering impression of the figure is not an end in itself; its purpose rather is to make prominent, like a picture through its precious frame, the main thing: the little open scroll in the angel's right hand. If the scroll is especially specified as being little, this means that it contains only a partial message from out of the book with the seven seals which contains the entire plan of salvation; the big scroll has in the meantime been completely opened (8 : 1), hence this part of it is no longer sealed either. Yet before the angel gives the Seer the little scroll with its inscribed message he hears him call out with a sound-volume which corresponding to his size John can only compare with the roar of a lion, a traditional image for an all-penetrating call (cf. Hos. 11 : 10; Amos 3 : 8).

³ᵇ... *when he called out, the seven thunders sounded.*

The loud call of the angel, which echoes from high up over the entire earth, is answered by a sevenfold echo, " the seven thunders "; they are supplied with the definite article, hence something definite and familiar must be meant by them. Thunder is used variously in the Bible as an image to describe the voice of God (Ps. 18[17] : 14; 29[28] : 3; Jer. 25 : 30f.; Jn. 12 : 28f.); hence it is uppermost in one's mind to regard the thunder as the answer of God to the call of the angel; the apocalyptic symbolism of the number seven would confirm this assumption.

⁴*And when the seven thunders had sounded, I was about to write, but I heard a voice from heaven saying, Seal up what the seven thunders have said, and do not write it down.*

The Seer obviously understood what the angel had called out and what the thunders had answered, for, in line with an earlier received commission (1 : 19), he wants to write it down. But in this case God expressly forbids it and thereby prohibits the publication of what was heard. Not all and everything is meant for each and everyone; there are also revelations of God which are given for entirely personal illumination and comfort (cf. 2 Cor. 12:4). He who is chosen by God as mediator of his salvific truth and its execution also obtains from him special supernatural insights and graces to fulfill this calling.

⁵And the angel whom I saw standing on the sea and land lifted up his right hand to heaven ⁶and swore by him who lives for ever and ever, who created heaven and what is in it, the earth and what is in it, and the sea and what is in it, that there should be no more delay, ⁷but that in the days of the trumpet call to be sounded by the seventh angel, the mystery of God, as he announced to his servants the prophets, should be fulfilled.

Once more the Seer draws the powerful figure of the angel in order to lay stress on what he now does; the presentation unmistakably relies on a text from Daniel (Dan. 12:7). With a solemn oath by the eternal creator of the universe the angel announces that the " mystery of God," that is, the salvific plan of God for his world, which had been hidden in him from eternity (cf. Eph. 3:9) and began to come to light with the creation, will now be completely fulfilled at the seventh trumpet call. The complete fulfillment of the promise of salvation, which God in revelation had entrusted as good news to his messengers for dissemination, will now no longer tolerate deferment. The oath of the angel, and its contents, aims to establish the faithful in the hope, and gladden them in the assurance which God solemnly guarantees them (cf. Lk. 21:28): world history, even in its darkest epochs, moves unerringly towards its goal which is God himself.

8Then the voice which I heard from heaven spoke to me again, saying, Go, take the scroll which is open in the hand of the angel who is standing on the sea and on the land. 9So I went to the angel and told him to give me the little scroll; and he said to me, Take it and eat; it will be bitter to your stomach, but sweet as honey in your mouth.

The angel has a further message to give John personally. The command to accept it comes from heaven; God's callings all come directly from God. The angel discharges his message with an action which is similar to the one whereby God laid the destiny of the world into the hands of the exalted Son of man who had redeemed it (5:7). The command personally to assimilate the imparted message in order then to make it known to others, is given him with equal drama as was experienced by the prophet Ezekiel at his calling (Ezek. 2:8–3:3). In the image of eating the basic pre-condition and essential character of all dissemination is aptly illustrated: its subject is not one's own thoughts but God's revelation; the prophet must assimilate them, without concision of content, as a personal testimony (" witness ") to people of his time and in terms of their world of ideas and modes of thought.

10And I took the little scroll from the hands of the angel and ate it; it was sweet as honey in my mouth, but when I had eaten it my stomach was made bitter. 11And I was told, You must again prophesy about many peoples and nations and tongues and kings.

The effect of this calling is ambiguous as the angel had already foretold. It is an honor to be elected a prophet by God and thus to become a confidant of his thoughts and intentions. But their content is not only grace but also justice. Hence the knowledge of God's will leaves a bitter aftertaste, also the bitter experiences in the exercise of the prophet's office have entered into this feature of the image (cf. Jer. 11:21; 15:10-21; 20:7-18). The vocation already executed in the symbolic action is in conclusion also put into words; the calling itself is here announced as a duty ("you must "). The reference to the universal content of the message lets one conclude that not only the immediately following visions (11:1-2), at least not in their narrowest interpretation, are the subject of the new revelation.

The Measuring of the Temple (11:1-2)

The interlude, which prepares for the disclosure of the seventh trumpet call, is continued with a vision in which a measuring of the temple is described; after that there is talk of the appearance of two witnesses in the " holy city " occupied by the heathen. Above all, the second part of this section appears very obscure at first sight; the darkness is dispelled somewhat when its position in the framework of the whole is taken into consideration.

Through the handing over of the little scroll John received a second special calling for the vision of the final phase of the history of salvation whose inception was expected with the seventh trumpet; likewise he was given a new task (cf. 1:11) not to withhold from the Church the terrifying images of this final combat (10:11). What was imparted to him in this respect he must reveal in what follows.

Before the breaking of the seventh seal, with which the end was to be expected, an interlude was inserted (7:1-17), which aimed at preparing the faithful for what was coming and giving them courage to endure the expected aggravation of ordeals. Evidently, the preliminary vision to the seventh trumpet call pursues the same purpose. This conjecture grows into a practical certainty when one compares the double vision of those receiving the seal with the two images here; their correspondence, in other words, extends not only to the tenor of their contents, it reaches to their formal construction. The measuring of the temple (11 : 1f.) is parallel in meaning with the sealing (7 : 1–8): both cases deal with protective measures for the faithful; and in the story of the two witnesses (11 : 3–13), in spite of the emphasis on the difficulty of their fight, their supernatural support in the fulfillment of their task and their final redemption remains the dominant motif; so here, too, the protection motif is transformed into the victory motif (11 : 11–13), which constitutes the second part of the " sealing " vision (7 : 9–17).

¹Then I was given a measuring rod like a staff, and I was told : Rise and measure the temple of God and the altar and those who worship there, ²but do not measure the court outside the temple; leave that out, for it is given over to the nations, and they will trample over the holy city for forty-two months.

As in the case of the angel in 7 : 2f. so here the Seer himself is told to perform a symbolic action; he is given a measuring rod with the command to measure a definite area of the temple precinct. Besides the reminder of the in-the-meantime destroyed temple of Jerusalem, two Old Testament models (Ezek. 40 : 3— 43 : 17; Zech. 2 : 5–9) have outwardly influenced the construction of the image. According to their inner symbolic content, temple and action of the Seer illustrate a definite end of time situation of the new people of God which signifies an extreme danger for the Church of Jesus Christ through which, although decimated, it will with God's special help be preserved to the extent that it will remain intact in its essence (faith and cult) (cf. Mt. 16 : 18).

A comparison with the special protective measure of the sealing (7 : 1–8)—in the measuring too it is basically less a question of space than people—makes clear that the situation of the Church in the world has in the meantime become much more difficult and restricted; above all the directive to leave out a large area of the temple, that is, the Church, when measuring is a sign that God will not simply shield the Church from attack by her enemies; in the end, a numerically reduced, yet through the trial of combat innerly purified and stabilized group will persevere in the worship of God.

The image reveals as safe asylum, besides the actual temple house with the two rooms, sanctuary and holy of holies, also the inner court in whose center the altar of burnt-offering stood; on the other hand, from the temple precinct, the great outer court and the " holy city," that is, Jerusalem (cf. Is. 48:2; Dan. 9:24; Mt. 27:53) in its entire circumference is left to the enemy to devastate.

As a symbol of the Church the temple precinct would have sufficed metaphorically; if then in addition a second symbolic image, not quite like the first, appears here, namely, the " holy city," then we can accept that it also conveys a special meaning. It suggests itself that the double symbol indicates the twofold relationship of the Church, to God and to the world; in analysis, this results in the acceptable meaning: the Church will lose entirely her cultural-profane position in the world, which in any case does not immediately belong to her mission and be pressed back into a " sacristy Christianity " with a further decimation in personnel by a mass-apostasy (the exclusion of the outer court); the latter would coincide with other places in the New Testament which contain this type of apocalyptic prophecy (Mt. 24:10–12; 2 Thess. 2:3).

The synoptic apocalypse also refers to such " times of the gentiles " which last until they are " fulfilled " (Lk. 21:24); this is what is here expressed by the definite time specification. The detail: 42 months (11:2; 13:5)=1,260 days (11:3; 12:6)=3½

years (12:14) relies on the book of Daniel where the duration
of the terrible dominion of Antiochus IV Epiphanes over Jerusalem is specified as lasting " a time, two times and a half a time "
(Dan. 7:25; 12:7) and "half a week " (Dan. 9:27), hence in
each case as 3½, that is, half a week of years = 3½ years. The
halved seven, in apocalyptic literature the evil measure of God's
foes, also appears in John's Revelation as the time-span of the
dominion of forces hostile to God; considering that seven means
completion (cf. 1:4), the most important symbolic expression of
the broken seven seems to be that all forces hostile to God
always come to a halt on the way to their intended goal. Hence
this last detail of the second image of the preliminary vision once
more underlines the real meaning of the entire interlude: despite
great distress from the outside and inside during " apocalyptic "
epochs of her history, the Church will be preserved and protected
by God himself in her inner essence and true domain. Certainly,
one ought not ignore the warning in this vision against all
attempts in difficult times to see the Church through with com-
promises at the expense of the whole truth and of unambiguous
piety, as well as the judgment passed here in anticipation on
every kind of mere borderline and cultural Christianity.

The Two Witnesses (11:3-13)

[3]*And I will grant my two witnesses power to prophesy for one
thousand two hundred and sixty days, clothed in sackcloth.*

Even in the epochs of greatest impairment, in respect to the
practical displacement from public life, the Church will not in
self-sufficiency shut herself off in a ghetto imposed from outside;
rather, despite the greatest threats she will, confident in the
protection of the Almighty, continue to fulfill her missionary
charge in, and for the world. This fact is foretold in the image
of the two witnesses and unfolded in an allegoric-symbolic

manner. Because it is the Church's most eminent task to preserve the witness to Jesus (cf. 6:9; 12:11. 17; 19:10) and to
preach it to mankind of all places and all ages (cf. Mt. 28:18f.),
the two representatives of believers in Christ, in the midst of a
world which has become ungodly, are called simply witnesses.
In line with the literary usage, occurring in antiquity and also
frequently in the Old Testament writings, of symbolically representing and characterizing communities, as for instance a city,
in fictitious personifications we will to begin with have to interpret the two witnesses as symbols of the Church as a whole.

The fact that there are two witnesses is not meant to differ-
entiate them since all pronouncements as to their appearance
and powers are true of both witnesses alike. Externally, the
number two could be due to a dependence on a text in the
prophet Zechariah (Zech. 4:2–14), elements from which John
used freely otherwise, transforming them into an independent
picture. Probably on the basis of an ancient judicial proverb,
" If of witnesses there are two, what they say will be true "
(cf. Deut. 19:15; Mt. 18:16; 2 Cor. 13:1; Tim. 5:19), the
duplication intends to give a special prominence to their credi-
bility in particular. The main content of their witness is the
prophetic call to repentance as indicated by their clothes (the
garment of mourning and penance; cf. Gen. 37:34; Is. 27:1;
58:5; Mt. 11:21) and which can also be inferred from the
situation in which they appear. Hence the Church will not allow
the call to repentance, even during the time in which the " holy
city " is given over to the heathens (cf. the corresponding time
specification in the verses 2 and 3), that is, in the epoch of the
mass-apostasy of believers, to grow silent.

*These are two olive trees and two lampstands which stand before
the Lord of the earth.*

In the model text of the prophet Zechariah the one olive tree symbolizes the high priest, the other the king; the lampstand occurs only once there, it has seven arms and indicates Yahweh's omniscience. High priest and king, the summit of Israel's religious and worldly authority, were anointed (" olive trees ") as a sign that they exercised their office in representation of, and with the full authority of Yahweh. This is also true of the two witnesses; their task is, therefore, more closely characterized as priestly and regally like that of the whole Church (cf. 1:6; 5:10); the lampstand comparison describes their function as light-bearers of divine truth in the eclipse of God of the completely profaned city. The anointed and the commissioned of the Lord are also under his special protection (" before the Lord of the earth ") in doing their official task.

⁵And if any one would harm them, fire pours from their mouth and consumes their foes; if any one would harm them, thus he is doomed to be killed. ⁶They have power to shut the sky, that no rain may fall during the days of their prophesying, and they have power over the waters to turn them into blood, and to smite the earth with every plague, as often as they desire.

In order to discharge their duty in hostile surroundings God has equipped them with miraculous powers for their own protection and as a testimony to the truth of their preaching. No human or demonic power can harm the Church or impede its activity against God's will; as a sign of contradiction like their Lord and Master (cf. Lk. 2:34) there is revealed in them as it was in him the powerlessness of the mighty and the might of the powerless through God, the omnipotent. Their word strikes back at those who reject it, who blaspheme and fight against it. All who harm the Church in the exercise of its mission suffer the fate of the foes of Elijah (2 Kings 1:9–14) and of Moses (Num. 16:25–35); in accordance with a known prophetic-figurative turn of speech (cf. Jer. 5:14; Is. 11:4), the threat is formulated that a word of power from the mouths of the witnesses will destroy them. But God does not only marvelously protect the person of his witnesses, he also makes possible their undisturbed activity through supernatural help by granting them the miraculous powers of Elijah (3 Kings 17 : 1; cf. Lk. 4 : 25; Jas. 5 : 17) and of Moses (Ex. 7 : 14–12 : 33). The various details of the image are meant to impress on the mind that no power of the world or underworld is capable of wiping out the Church or neutralizing its witness; she will survive even the greatest peril.

The question now arises whether the symbolism of the two witnesses is exhausted in this general reference to the Church as such, or whether a further symbolism, which necessitates a further special interpretation, is intended. The formulation: " my two witnesses " introduces them it seems as two specific, known persons. Their description is linked with details from the life and work of Moses and Elijah; these were regarded as the embodiment of the " law and the prophets " (cf. Mt. 5 : 17; 7 : 12 i.a.) and therefore also appear at the transfiguration of Jesus (Mt. 17 : 3). There is a tradition in Judaism that Elijah would return at the end of time before the great judgment day of God (Mal. 3 : 23; Mt. 11 : 10. 14; Mk. 6 : 5; 9 : 11–13; Jn. 1 : 21). Moreover, on the basis of an old promise (Deut. 18 : 15) the opinion arose that the prophet mentioned there would appear before the coming of the Messiah (cf. " the prophet ": Jn. 1 : 21; 6 : 14; 7 : 40). Hence in the description one of the witnesses is provided with characteristics from the story of Elijah and the other from the story of Moses.

Although Revelation has linked with the two witnesses still another interpretation beyond that of symbolizing the Church as such relating to two individual personalities, it does not, however, refer to these historical men in person; the entire description seems rather to indicate that there are two prophets appearing before the end of time who are equipped with the " spirit

and power " of these great men in the history of Israel (cf. Lk.
1:17; Mt. 11:10. 14). The decision in this question depends on
how the passage (11:3–13) is to be judged according to type and
content in the framework of the entire composition. To be pre-
cise, this section does not portray a vision in the actual sense of
the word; rather, by means of various elements taken from later
visions and sufficiently clear in their context (cf. 11:7 with
13:1ff.), a prophecy is made only which anticipates, for the purpose of calming and encouraging, the happy ending to a difficult
ordeal. Depending on whether one sees the animal from the
bottomless pit in 13:1ff. as an individual (the " antichrist "), the
same will have to be said of the witnesses whom the beast kills.
The continuation of their description in what follows seems to
favor the assumption that the prophecy of our text, although
certainly to begin with it describes quite generally the fate of
the Church during the final time, in addition promises, for the
especially difficult situation before the end of time, two concrete
prophetic figures who will stand by the Church in its combat
with the equally concrete figure of the antichrist.

*7And when they have finished their testimony, the beast that
ascends from the bottomless pit will make war upon them and
conquer them and kill them, 8and their dead bodies will lie in
the street of the great city which is allegorically called Sodom
and Egypt, where the Lord was crucified.*

When God considers their time fulfilled, the final fate of the two
witnesses and the termination of their testimony is sealed by the
beast from the bottomless pit. This detail concerning his origin
characterizes the beast as a demonic power; the definite article
most probably indicates that the beast is introduced as an individual known to the first readers of Revelation. With the appearance of the beast, described in detail in the Chapters 13 and 17,

world history seems now to end in the total triumph of evil; the victory of the antichrist over the Church of Christ seems now to be complete. Her witnesses die the death of martyrs and the hatred of their foes seems to pursue them even beyond death; their bodies are dishonored by the refusal of burial. The place of their ministry the " holy city " (11:2), relinquished to the heathen, is now after the wicked deed called " the great city," as later Babylon, the capital city of the antichrist (cf. 16:19; 17:18; 18:10.16-21). How things now are in the city and what happens there is suggested by the " symbolically " intended names: Sodom and Egypt. Sodom serves prophetic literature as the archetype of moral degradation (cf. Is. 1:9; 3:9; Ezek. 16:46-50) and Egypt is a type of tyranny and imperviousness (Wis. 19:13-17).

The additional remark concerning the crucifixion of Jesus is here too, like everything else, to be understood symbolically. In the image of Jerusalem—at the beginning of the interlude (11:1-2) initially a symbol for the interrelation of world and Church—John had presented the banishment of the Church from the world; the city district and part of the temple precinct came into the possession of the enemy. The fact that the Lord was crucified in the historical Jerusalem is taken by the Seer as an opportunity for the assertion that the same powers who were the cause of Jesus' death are also at work behind the persecution of his Church. Jesus' death is set forth in the martyrdom of his faithful; already in the oldest documents of Christian theology the Church is defined as the body of Christ in its essence to which the faithful belong as members (Rom. 12:4f.; 1 Cor. 6:15; 10:16f.; 12:12-14; Eph. 1:23f., etc.).

⁹For three days and a half men from the peoples and tribes and tongues and nations gaze at their dead bodies and refuse to let them be placed in a tomb, ¹⁰and those who dwell on the earth rejoice over them and make merry and exchange presents, because these two prophets had been a torment to those who dwell on the earth.

How completely the sovereignty of the beast has been established over mankind is demonstrated by the fact that all the people of the world (classified according to the cosmic number four) rejoice as if liberated and, as on great feast days, exchange presents after the mouths of these prophets had been struck dumb. The demand for repentance which God had voiced through them was experienced as a nuisance and torment; as if awakened out of a nightmare " those who dwell on the earth " (cf. 6:10) breathe again freely. A disturbing thought, that the gospel can be conceived as a torment and that mankind celebrates festivals because God is silent and hell alone has leave to speak. However, the total triumph of evil is only of short duration (three and a half days—the shortest measure of time for wickedness); the sensation of being able to gaze on the corpses of the prophets as trophies of victory is short-lived.

11But after the three and a half days a breath of life from God entered them, and they stood upon their feet, and great fear fell on those who saw them. 12Then they heard a loud voice from heaven saying to them, Come up hither! And in the sight of their foes they went up to heaven in a cloud. 13And at that hour there was a great earthquake, and the rest were terrified and gave glory to the God of heaven.

Just as the crucified Christ rose after three days and silenced the triumph of his foes so it happened with these two who " bore witness to Jesus " (cf. 6:9; 12:17; 20:4); God stands by his two witnesses (1:3) as he did by his " faithful witness " Jesus (cf. 1:5; 3:14), and in the same manner, since they also sealed their loyalty by death. With reference to elements from the resurrection prophecy of Ezekiel (Ezek. 37:5. 10), John describes their awakening from the dead. The occurrence of their resuscitation as well as their subsequent assumption into heaven takes place, in contrast with the same event in the life of Jesus, before the eyes of their terrified foes. God has shown himself stronger in them than all the might of the beast with whom the masses had taken side; the jubilation of " those who dwell on earth " therefore abruptly reverses into fear and terror for they sense God's judgment which is then immediately announced in a natural phenomenon. As at the resurrection of Jesus, a great earthquake occurs (cf. Mt. 28:2) which lays a tenth of the city in ruins and buries a corresponding number of people under the rubble. The interlude ends with the consoling assertion that in consequence of what happened to the dead men that which they themselves had not achieved with their preaching actually occurs: the survivors come to their senses, the great defection from Christianity (cf. 11:2) is at an end and is reversed into conversion.

This positive observation confirms the inner unity of the sections 11:1-2 and 11:3-13. All plagues which have so far been inflicted on rebellious mankind by God ended in failure; here there is for the first time talk of conversion, a sign that the occurrences of this interlude intend to illustrate something unique in comparison with the plague-visions; already the choice of Jerusalem as a symbolic place for the events is remarkable and therefore surely significant. All these circumstances lead one to conclude that besides the threat to the Church from the outside the much more critical danger from within is here also implied. Certainly, threats from her own ranks are also repeated—by Christians who conform to this world (cf. Rom. 12:2) and thereby obscure the Church's image before the world—in the course of the Church's history as is also the recuperation from out of a good remainder which always survives, a kernel which has remained alive. The situation, however, which is presupposed in 11:1–13 is unrepeatable in so far as here without doubt the epoch of the antichrist is referred to which is only later portrayed in detail (13:1ff.). But even in case of the most serious existential crisis, which is caused, and marked, by the most vigorous pressures from outside as well as the spread of unbelief and moral decline within, the Church is promised in these descriptions and assured salvation by some extraordinary interventions of God. Hence this interlude has the same meaning as the one concerning the sealed ones (7:1–17) and just like the latter in its second part it anticipates later delineations, here above all the description of the antichrist (13:11–18), for which it intends especially to prepare and to arm against.

The Seventh Trumpet; The Third Woe (11:14–19)

¹⁴The second woe has passed; behold, the third woe is soon to come.

This verse aims to re-establish, after the interlude, the link with the trumpet cycle; in this transition-remark the second part of the sentence, which announces the imminence of the third woe with the seventh trumpet call, carries the stress; it does not therefore assert that the section 10:1–11:13 is to be reckoned with the second woe.

¹⁵Then the seventh angel blew his trumpet, and there were loud voices in heaven, saying, The kingdom of the world has become the kingdom of our Lord and of his Christ, and he shall reign for ever and ever. ¹⁶And the twenty-four elders who sit on their thrones before God fell on their faces and worshipped God, ¹⁷ saying, We give thanks to thee, Lord God Almighty, who art and who wast, that thou hast taken thy great power and begun to reign. ¹⁸The nations raged, but thy wrath came, and the time for the dead to be judged, for rewarding thy servants, the

prophets and saints, and those who fear thy name, both small
and great, and for destroying the destroyers of the earth.

With the seventh trumpet-call, according to the angel's word
(10:6f.), time has come to an end, the "secret of God," his
eternal plan of salvation is brought to its goal; the kingdom of
God now begins to be fully established in God's creation. The
description of the last woe, preparation and execution of the
final judgment, is skipped to begin with; first we hear with a
cry of joy from heaven that world history has come to an end
with the perfect establishment of God's kingdom over the universe for all eternity; God's kingdom is now established for
ever and it can be experienced once more from the outside, that
is, it has become a tangible reality for all his creatures. This
glimpse of the future, which reminds one in type and content
of 7:9–17 and evidently also pursues the same purpose, adds
the final re-enforcing point to the exhortation towards which the
whole interlude is tailored.

The representatives of the Church by the throne of God, the
"elders," celebrate the happy completion of God's creation with
a hymn of praise and thanksgiving; for now the battle is over,
which the Church, as the seed of God's kingdom sown into this
world, has had to endure in her history. The cause of this
combat, Satan, till now admitted as "ruler of this world"
(Jn. 12:31) by God, no longer has a place in the new world of
God; he and his followers have been judged. God, the "Almighty who is and was," has come—hence the third part,
"who is to come" (cf. 1:8; 4:8) is missing—and has sat in
judgment on all the destroyers of his creation; the patience
which he has so long shown towards them—a sign of his absolute superiority and power—was often enough a stumbling-block
for his loyal ones and had been no small trial to their faith; they
have passed the test and are now being rewarded far beyond
their deserts.

[19a]*Then God's temple in heaven was opened, and the ark of his covenant was seen within his temple; . . .*

After John has merely heard of the reward of the just in the song of the elders, he is in the end shown it through a vision in a symbolic process, still in its present location, and with it the blessed final goal of everything there is. Heaven opens before his eyes, depicted as the temple of Jerusalem in which Yahweh at one time had been present in the midst of his chosen people on earth. John can look as far in as the holy of holies and there he sees the ark of the covenant, the place of God's presence in the sanctuary of Israel. In this shrine were kept the documents and pledges of the provisional first covenant which according to God's salvific intentions were to be a model of, and a preparation for the new and eternal Covenant with which the history of salvation concludes. This new covenant, the direct and ever-lasting fellowship of God with his people of the new covenant, has now become reality in a blessed consummation. The detailed delineation of this reality, announced here in substance, constitutes the climax and conclusion of the apocalyptic prophecy (21 : 1–22 : 5).

[19b]*and there were flashes of lightning, loud noises, peals of thunder, an earthquake, and heavy hail.*

Just as God's presence means bliss to his faithful, it spreads terror among his foes. With presentiments of the coming judgment (earthquake, thunder-storm) the presentation moves from the prospect of the final outcome back again to the beginning of the final phase which was started with the last trumpet.